The Only 250
Letters and Memos
Managers Will
Ever Need

The Only 250 Letters and Memos Managers Will Ever Need

Ron Tepper

John Wiley & Sons, Inc.

New York • Chichester • Brisbane • Toronto • Singapore

Library of Congress Cataloging-in-Publication Data

Tepper, Ron, 1937–
    The only 250 letters and memos managers will ever need / by Ron
Tepper
        p.   cm.
    Includes bibliographical references.
    ISBN 0-471-52459-X
    1. Commercial correspondence. 2. Memorandums.   I. Title.
HF5721.T44   1990
658.4'53—dc20   89-78148
                                                   CIP

Printed in the United States of America

91 10 9 8 7 6 5 4 3 2

To Janet,

the most prolific letter and memo writer in the business

Contents

The Only 250
Letters and Memos
Managers Will
Ever Need

Introduction

My Dear Friend:

No doubt you will be madly surprised on receipt of this Epistle. But nevertheless I could not resist the temptation and hope if you cannot do me the great favor of dropping me a few lines you will at least excuse me for this for I can't help it.

The opening lines on the previous page begin a letter written more than a half-century ago by humorist Will Rogers. Rogers viewed letter writing as the epitome of communication; however, he would be amazed at how the art of letter and memo writing has changed throughout America.

In Rogers's day, good letter and memo writers were abundant. The written word was king. In today's society, however, video and the spoken word rule, while well-constructed business letters and memos are becoming rare. To some, writing one good follow-up sales letter or internal memo is more difficult than working a 40-hour week.

That shouldn't be. Almost all well-constructed letters adhere to a four-step formula. Master the formula, which is detailed in this book, and letter and memo writing becomes quick and painless rather than drudgery. For the businessperson who adheres to the formula, good letters can be written almost as quickly as the words are spoken.

Letter writers do not have to be college graduates, either. All that is required is mastery of the four-step process. Once those steps are mastered, the businessperson will find that letter writing is not only quick, but it also gives him or her the chance to be creative—and to increase sales.

Eighteen companies volunteered sales correspondence, memos, and other written documents for this book. (In return for their correspondence it was agreed that the names of clients would not be used, nor would any company letterhead.) Each of the companies practices good letter and memo writing, and most use the four-step process.

For these companies, good letter writing equates to higher sales volume, better internal communication, and more productive employees. For example, several pointed out that the typical salesperson has less time than ever to call on accounts. That holds true whether the business is manufacturing or service. Time has become a premium to business. Yet repeat business depends on contact between sales and customer. In fact, *post-purchase selling*, which means the amount of additional products or services a customer purchases after the initial buy, can account for as much as 50 percent of a firm's sales. But that business never comes through the door if there is a lack of communication.

By utilizing written communication, many firms have enabled salespeople to increase communication, to build a campaign where every month, or at least every quarter, the customer gets some kind of correspondence. This correspondence keeps the company and the salesperson on the mind of the customer. These letters can be planned and programmed into computers and mailed on the first of the month or on the first day of a new quarter. These include specialized letters (outlined in Chapter 4) that contain information and educational material and make an indirect sales pitch. These letters pay major dividends for the companies that are using them.

The same is true of memos. Although most memos are used internally (within the company), a growing number of salespeople are writing short personalized notes (memos) to clients and thereby increasing the amount of communication between clients and prospects. Even internally, memos have taken on new importance. With the busy schedule of most executives, memos are increasingly being used to recap meetings, document decisions, outline campaigns, and pinpoint responsibilities.

Together, letters and memos have not only taken on a new importance in the workplace, but they also have become critical tools for companies as they approach the twenty-first century.

CHAPTER 1

Rules and Format

Dear Cerf:

By some miracle you have published a book which is not second rate. Please send me twelve copies at once.

Yours sincerely,
A. Woolcott

Dear Woolcott:

By some miracle you can buy those twelve copies at Brentano's.

Yours Very Truly,
Bennett Cerf

The letter from writer Alexander Woolcott to his friend, Bennett Cerf (and the return note from Cerf) are not only classics in letter writing, but also examples of why good letter and memo writing is an art, as well as a superior communication device. In contrast to many letters, the Woolcott–Cerf exchange reveals the personalities of two men, each with a tremendous sense of humor. The letters also reveal that the pair were old friends who did not hesitate to deprecate each other with well-placed barbs.

Woolcott and Cerf demonstrate one other thing about good letters—they do not have to be long to get the message across. Good letters and memos are crisp and clear, as are good conversations and good speeches. Good letters and memos have definite trademarks. For example, in Woolcott's initial note, only three words contain more than one syllable. In Cerf's, only two do. Letters that are brief and highlighted by monosyllabic words characterize good communicators. Short and to the point. The sentences do not run on and are not overly long. That also happens to be the way most of us talk when speaking with business associates, and we should be writing the same way.

Businesspeople who communicate perfectly when speaking to someone across the room frequently tighten up and put in excess verbiage when writing a simple note or memo. For some reason, many believe words on paper should be adorned with as many adjectives and adverbs as possible. Although adjectives and adverbs certainly have a place in communication, the best letters and memos are simple and straightforward. The adjectives and adverbs that are used are well-placed and appropriate. An example of simplicity and communication at its best is the following memo, written by the marketing director of a West Coast real estate firm. The memo announces a new member in the department.

It is with great pleasure that I announce we've traded two players and a future draft choice to Jim _____, Wes _____, and Shelley _____ for speedy Jeanne _____. Jeanne is being promoted to the first string—the marketing department—where she will be the Marketing PR coordinator beginning Nov. 1.

In her new position, Jeanne will deal with the media, assist in the preparation of the company newsletter, market softening and PR campaigns, write brochures and use her many marketing talents on a variety of assignments.

Jeanne started with _____ in February, 1988, as _____ for _____.

Our thanks to Jim, Shelly and Wes for developing and supplying us with this #1 draft choice.

The preceding example, while refreshing and interesting, is not intended to suggest that every letter and memo has to be humorous. Correspondence should, however, be written to keep the reader's interest. Letters and memos should also convey the personality of the person, department, or company writing them.

A personnel memo announcing the appointment of a new employee need not be loaded with clichés. It can have color and flair. The memo written by the marketing department is creative and down-to-earth and fits the image of the department. It may not, however, fit other departments (e.g., data processing) within the company. Memo writers have to make that judgment and ask themselves, "What is the image of our department? What is appropriate and what isn't?"

Memos should also reflect the entire company's personality. Is the company formal? Informal? Is it a mature, well-established Fortune 500 company, or is it a free swinging, new young enterprise? Is it a bank or bowling alley? An auto manufacturer or automatic car wash? Regardless of the business, where is room for creativity. Some memos suit the image of both a formal and an informal company. Memo 1–1 can be used for either type of company.

THINK ABOUT THE AUDIENCE

Jay Abraham, a talented marketing entrepreneur who makes a large portion of his living through his ability with the spoken word, admon-

```
Date:

To:

From:

Subject:    Promotion

I am please to announce the promotion of
[name] to Programmer/Analyst.

[Name] has been with us since [date] as a
Senior Programmer. He [she] has been
instrumental in our computer division's
development since we opened for business last
March. He [she] has also been the project
leader for Release 2.10.

[Name] will continue to help in the creation
and ongoing development of our computer
product.

Please join me in congratulating [name] on his
[her] promotion, and on wishing him [her]
continued success.

signed

JH/ib
```

Memo 1–1: A personnel memo suitable for a formal or an informal company.

ishes letter writers to think about the audience: "What will interest them? How should it be said? How do you get the message across so they remember it?"

Abraham supplied two examples of letters that were the backbone of a successful marketing campaign. The first went to consumers, the second to publishers (Letters 1–1 and 1–2).

Although the letters go to different markets, they have several key elements in common—elements that every letter writer should follow regardless of the subject and audience. First, the language in both letters talks directly to the recipient. They are targeted at the reader's (not the writer's) needs. Their physical format is similar, too. They both have short, punchy paragraphs that make each letter readable. The paragraph indentation also keep the reader's eyes moving down the page.

Well-structured and well-written correspondence can be one of the most important things a businessperson does. A letter with a touch of humor can win over a prospective client. It says to the recipient that the originator is more than black ink on white paper. He or she has a personality, and in letter and memo writing, it is just as important to convey a covert meaning as an overt one.

Well-written memos tell employees that the boss is human; he or she is one of them. Compare Memos 1–2 and 1–3. Each gives a mental picture of management.

Memo 1–2 leaves no doubt that management is tough, business-like, and adversarial. The only question is whether management cares at all for the employees. The same message could have been put across with far less acrimony. Correspondence such as this is not new to the business world.

Memo 1–3 is about an equally serious topic; however, management has put together a memo that asks employees for their cooperation and shows that the company cares as well. Obviously, one of the company's primary concerns regarding worker compensation claims is the cost, but dollars lost (to the company) is not something that impacts employees as much as a plea from management that says, "We care about you."

George Post, chief executive officer (CEO) of one of the most successful independent banks in the country, says "letter and memo writing has become a lost art." Post knows. Some of his prose is among the best ever penned in the world of finance. His correspondence is also a lesson in brevity that every businessperson would be wise to learn.

Dear Friend:

I'd like to take a minute of your time to talk about an extremely important subject: your health!

No one can possibly take your health as seriously as you do.

Perhaps I am responsible for gently "pushing" you to improve your nutritional intake—but now it's up to you to take full control of your nutritional requirements. You alone must sustain and perpetuate the benefits you'll receive from starting to take the A.M./P.M. solution.

It's an investment in your body that will pay dividends for many years to come.

The benefits of having proper nutritional balance within your body include looking better, feeling better, and having more energy, more concentration, and less tension. I honestly believe that once you get your body nutritionally balanced, you'll transform yourself into the healthiest, strongest, most alive person you can be.

To help guide you in the investment you've made in your own health, I've included a handy reference guide to the vitamins and minerals contained in the A.M./P.M. solution.

The reference guide explains the importance of each ingredient I've chosen to include in the A.M./P.M. supplement. It also clearly explains why that ingredient is vital for you to include in your diet every day.

It's essential for you to be fully informed on the purpose of each vitamin within the body—as well as knowing the consequences a deficiency can lead to. Only then can you take full control and responsibility for your health.

I hope this reference guide will serve to keep you motivated to take your A.M. and your P.M. solution each and every day. It should serve as a daily reminder of the vital need your body has for the vitamins and minerals in the A.M./P.M. supplement. You see, it's often the case that, after reaping short-term rewards, people suddenly stop taking their vitamin supplements, because they "feel better."

Letter 1–1: A successful marketing letter to customers.

When you notice an improvement in your health, don't stop! Continue with what works!

Our experience has shown that it's best to establish a routine for taking your supplement—integrate it as another essential part of your daily life, like brushing your teeth, and you'll best be able to see the benefits nutritional balance can accrue for you. Setting a specific time (say, for example, 8:00 A.M. in the morning and 6:30 at night) can assist you in maintaining this healthful pattern of life.

Your spouse and your family should soon notice the improvement, and probably will begin commenting on the great change (for the better!) that's come over you.

When they do (and I'm confident they will), keep in mind that sound nutritional balance (by taking your A.M./P.M. supplement daily) can maintain that "turn for the better" for a long, long time to come.

Of course, it will take a little time for the benefits of nutritional balance to take effect. Don't forget that years of poor nutrition, imbalanced diet, fast food, and vitamin and/or mineral deficiency require some time to correct. But once you start whittling away at that imbalance—you won't believe the amazing new you that is possible!

The reference guide is an introduction to helping you monitor how you feel from day to day. It's essential that you pay close attention to the signals your body is sending you—listen to your body—and you will have taken a giant step towards good health and a longer life.

Please write to tell me about the improvement in your health (both mental and physical) and your general sense of vitality. I'm genuinely interested.

Warmly,

Letter 1–1: *(continued)*

Dear Publisher:

You can add an extra $2,000 to $25,000 per issue to your magazine's bottom line without any effort or investment on your part—and without any risk either.

By developing the ancillary profit opportunities available through your publication, you can easily generate enough extra cash flow to provide you the means to do any of a number of critical projects you've been putting off—such as hiring new editors or salesmen or just having the necessary cash flow to comfortably meet payables expense.

I'll develop, operate, administer and implement these profit centers for you on a joint venture basis, splitting all revenues with you 50-50. Remember, we're talking about income you'd never have access to if we didn't develop it for you.

What kind of programs am I talking about? These, for example.

Creation of a special product and service section in the back of the magazine where we offer 5–12 different, exclusive and expensive independent learning products (like manuals and courses) that are not readily available to your readers. These would only be quality collections of relevant information and they would never be products that would be run in your "paid" advertising pages—so we would never take ad revenue away from you.

Typically, we would offer a broad spectrum of products covering such wide, but timely, subjects as personal investment, real estate, marketing, advertising, promotion, financial management, cash-flow management, etc. Of course the specific products we'd offer would be pre-screened by you and selected on the basis of their suitability to your specific readers. But you needn't worry because we have literally 1,000 different products available to select from.

Let me go on.

Once we pick out the products we want to offer I'll create appropriate copy and we'll run it in a double truck section

Letter 1–2: A successful marketing letter to publishers.

under the banner title of "Special Product Review" or some other designation that conveys valuable new products.

Typically, these products will sell for $25 to $195. Again, you will pre-approve each item so you have total control over price points we offer. We make between 30 and 50% on each item and every product we offer is of high enough quality that I have no problem offering them for purchase on an unconditional, money-back basis to your readers.

I've engineered a number of house product centers like this for newsletters, and years ago I did the same for two prominent magazines.

They produced between $10,000 and $200,000 an issue.

Of course, depending on your demographic profile and circulation size, we might only produce a few thousand dollars an issue in revenues. But then, again, if your market is highly responsive and your readership is large, we could do much, much better.

Either way, I am willing to develop this profit center for you totally at my risk. I'll spend the time and money finding the right products for your readers. I'll write all the copy. I'll typeset all the copy. I'll handle order processing, fulfillment, refunds (if any) and guarantee you a problem free operation.

All you do is allocate two pages a month to the venture until I prove the concept's extraordinary profitability, at which time I hope you'll allocate extra pages if required.

By the way, just because you've never done anything like this before does not mean it won't prove tremendously successful. By concentrating on timely and exclusive learning products that are relatively high priced, it doesn't require much response in terms of number of orders to make a lot of money. Also, by selecting products that appeal to your readers, then writing the ad copy totally for them, we amplify the responses to the concept many times.

But, in case you are somewhat apprehensive, I'm quite willing to set up a simple trial arrangement to help you gauge the potential profit such a venture can provide for you. Just

Letter 1–2: *(continued)*

agree to allow me two successive issues to try out. If it doesn't produce a minimum amount of profit to you during that time (we'll decide what that amount should be when we talk), don't continue the project.

If it does produce the profit I hope for, I ask only that you agree to continue the project in partnership with me for the next 12 months. After that, if you prefer doing it internally, I'm willing to let you do so and make all the money yourself. I only want a fair and reasonable chance to expose and develop a potentially valuable profit opportunity for you, and to benefit financially from my efforts.

As far as money management goes, we can do it one of two ways. Either all the money goes to you and you remit my share to me along with product costs, or I'll set up a trust account with instructions for your percentage of all gross monies deposited to be transferred to you every week.

Letter 1–2: *(continued)*

Date:

To:

From:

Subject: General Appearance

It has come to my attention that the manner of
dress in the office has been deteriorating.
From time to time, I have observed staff
dressed very casually—too casually for our
office, especially the front office.
Clothing such as sweatsuits, casual slacks,
and midriff-revealing outfits are not part of
a positive business image. We are an important
part of the business community, and you are an
important part of the image we project.

Employees are expected to present a neat,
businesslike appearance while at work.

Memo 1–2: A tough memo regarding employee dress.

Date:

To:

From:

Subject: Worker Compensation Injuries/Claims

During the first five months of this year, ten employee injuries were reported. Though none were serious, their occurrence causes concern. Each injury was preventable and, therefore, unnecessary.

Five accidents each were reported for the maintenance and child care departments. Most were due to dropping heavy objects on feet and running into sharp objects. These were certainly preventable.

Let's do everything we can to educate, train, and coach our staff to prevent injuries to themselves and to our program's participants. If you'd like to look at our monthly injury reports, they are available in the business office.

Thanks!

Memo 1–3: A caring memo discussing on-the-job injuries.

Dear Eduardo:

Assume you wish to renew your loan with us. My assumptions have historically been proven correct; however, I take no delight in my proximity to divinity. Please sign the enclosed papers and ship back.

Your humble servant,

George Post

Nice approach from a banker. The letter does more, however, than strike a humorous chord. Humor is not the goal of good letter and memo writers. Post's message also communicates that he is a banker with a personality and a sense of humor. Like the rest of us, he is human. The letter belies the myth that bankers are merely hard-nosed bean counters with steel hearts. It paints a desirable, warm image of Post. It shows that regardless of how formal a person's business may be, correspondence can be constructed to show employees, customers, and prospects that the letter writer is human; he or she does have a personality and warmth. This is especially important in situations where the letter writer is involved in a business that does not convey any warmth—a business such as banking. Compare Post's humorous note to Memo 1–4 and note how much more warmth and friendliness Post's document conveyed. Most important, note the picture it paints of Post versus the cold, impersonal portrait the memo leaves in the recipient's mind. (This memo, incidentally, was also written by a banker.)

Although he is a banker, Post knows it is important for him to communicate with his customers. His customers must feel comfortable in dealing with him. Thus, the letter to "Eduardo." Naturally, Eduardo is a customer known to Post. Even if the recipient is not known to the writer, every effort should be made to make him or her feel at home and comfortable in dealing with the company.

The letters from Woolcott, Cerf, Post, and Abraham not only convey messages, but also give readers an insight into the writer's personality, which is what every effective letter and memo should do.

WORKS OF ART

Good letters and memos are works of art. As most of us recognize, a work of art is not put together in a matter of minutes. Effective letter

Date:

To:

From:

Subject: Attendance Rating

It has come to my attention in reviewing recent performance evaluations for the secretarial and staff/clerical grades that managers are not using the Office Conduct Section (see Attendance, pages _____) in the Personnel Manual to guide their rating of an employee's attendance.

For example, two absences during the probationary period cannot be classified as an "average" rating. At best, this would be considered below average and at worst, it would require a warning, depending on the circumstances. Please consider the number of occurrences and review the attendance guidelines so that we are consistent in our rating policies. In this way, we can avoid employee complaints of preferential treatment.

It will be necessary for the personnel department to return performance evaluations to the managers if they reflect inconsistencies regarding attendance guidelines.

Thank you for your help.

Memo 1–4: A cold, impersonal memo concerning attendance.

and memo writers spend time on correspondence. They do not just jot thoughts down and send the letter out. Nor do they rely on a secretary to "write a note" to a client. They are economical, too. Good letter and memo writers subscribe to the adage that you say what you should say as quickly and simply as possible. That does not mean that long letters have no place in correspondence. The adage does mean, however, that if the letter is lengthy, it should be so because the writer is transmitting pertinent information, not just rambling.

Good letter and memo writers also subscribe to the cliché, "You never get a second chance to make a first impression." The first time you meet prospective clients or associates, they form immediate opinions based on what they see. Letters and memos have the same impact. For example, the first thing a customer sees from his or her banker is usually a bank statement. Post and others, however, make it a point to send a personal note to customers within a day or two after they have made their initial visit to the bank (Letter 1–3). The format and verbiage applies to many businesses, whether it is the holiday season or not. In a non-holiday season, the first six words could be replaced with "In the day-to-day running of our company." The second paragraph could be reworded as follows: "So lest we forget, thank you, and may this year be prosperous and rewarding for you and your company."

HOLD FOR 24 HOURS

With letters, recipients form an instantaneous impression based on (1) the envelope, (2) the letterhead, and (3) the content. Memos have the same impact. If the first impression is going to be favorable, letter and memo writers had better put as much time into their correspondence as they do into their grooming before meeting someone. Just as the executive on the way to an important meeting takes one last look in the mirror, letter and memo writers should take one last look at their correspondence.

If there is time, the astute letter and memo writer pens the correspondence, holds it for 24 hours, rereads it, revises, and then sends it. Take, for instance, the following letter, which was put together by a company vice president in the Midwest. His busy day had been interrupted by an irate customer complaining about the company's products. The irritated vice president finally

Dear   :

    As the holiday season draws near, there is so much activity and personal business to attend to that it is easy to forget to thank our valued customers, like you, for their patronage.

    We therefore wish now to thank you and to tell you we hope that this holiday season brings to you and your family joy and happiness now and throughout the new year.

            Cheers,

Letter 1–3: A personal follow-up letter combined with a holiday greeting.

got the consumer off the line and hurriedly wrote the following :

> I understand your problem; however, your complaint must go through channels. The regional director handles all problems of the type you described to me.

> I would suggest contacting [*name*] at [*number*]. I am sure he can help.

Fortunately, the executive had a habit of holding correspondence for a day before he sent it. When he reread his curt note the following morning, he immediately saw his mistake and rephrased it.

> Thank you for taking the time to let me know about problems you have been having with our [*product*].

> [*Name*] is our regional director in your area, and I have contacted him and told him what has been happening. You should be hearing from him by the end of the week, and I am sure the problem will be solved.

> Thank you, once again, for letting me know about the [*product problem*]. We'll be checking other models.

HANDLING CONSUMER COMPLAINTS

Consumer complaints are familiar to most companies. To brush off the customer is a mistake. The effect of one unhappy customer multiplies 100 times more rapidly than one who is satisfied. The vice president who wrote the preceding paragraphs knew that and realized his mistake because he took his correspondence seriously. Unfortunately, many executives do not. They would never ask another person to make a key oral presentation, but they trust others to write correspondence, and often to sign it.

For example, after a lengthy business session in which two parties come to a long-awaited agreement, the executive may ask his secretary to "write a cover letter" and send it with the contract. As a result, the warmth and rapport generated via lengthy meetings is often dissipated by a confirming letter that starts out with "Enclosed you will find . . ." It is as if the two parties never met.

Compare this opening with that in the following example, which was borrowed from the president of a marketing company who had just made a presentation to a prospective client.

Dear   :

Enjoyed meeting with you and [*name*] and particularly reminiscing about that ancient Notre Dame/Purdue game. I still say the Boilermakers could have pulled it out if they had had the time. Nevertheless, it was fun.

I've put together the material we discussed and I think you will find it measures up to what we were talking about. Read it over and see what you think. I will give you a call toward the end of next week.

And don't forget . . . the next time we meet during football season, let's try and work in a Boilermaker or an Irish game.

Notice the familiarity and friendliness. The note continues where the meeting left off—as it should. Letters should be a sales aid, not a sales deterrent. A salesperson writing a short note to a client should strive to include something personal (e.g., the football game, kids, school, or an old friend mentioned in their discussion).

LETTERS VERSUS CONVERSATION

Letters should be no different than a conversation with a business associate. Before the parties involved get down to business, they usually engage in small talk about a nonbusiness subject. The nonbusiness portion of the conversation helps the participants develop rapport. The same is true of letter writing. A friendly opening gives the recipient a sense of familiarity with the writer.

Often, a salesperson comes out of a lengthy presentation, goes back to his office and asks a secretary to write a "nice thank you note" to the prospect. The secretary has no idea as to what went on in the meeting and consequently the note can come off cold, aloof, like this:

Dear   :

I enjoyed meeting with you and your group this morning. I hope we can get together on the project. I'm in the process of putting together the plan we discussed and will get it to you as soon as possible.

All business letters are better when they are written by the person involved in the meeting or conference. The personal touch adds to correspondence. Just ask Bruce Webster. A few years ago, he was the owner of a small, struggling marketing firm that had garnered an excellent reputation for quality work. One day, he found himself making a presentation to one of the country's best-known political figures. He spent nearly two hours with the politician and was told that a decision would be made the following week.

Webster returned to his office and immediately did some thinking about what had transpired in the office. He had given the politician a number of ideas, but he also listened carefully to what the politician was saying. To his surprise, the young man indicated that one of his goals was to one day run for the U.S. Presidency. When Webster wrote his note, he kept that in mind:

Dear   :

Just a short note to express my appreciation for the time you took this morning.

I was impressed and excited about the goals you outlined and the plans you're formulating in order to reach them. Since returning, I have some ideas that definitely tie into your long-range plans. Perhaps, when you get some time, we can sit down and discuss them in depth.

I look forward to hearing from you and being part of the team.

Notice the conversational tone of Webster's note. His use of contractions helps make the note more familiar, and his mention of the politician's goals showed the prospective client that Webster was not just talking—he was listening. Webster also dropped a "tease"—"I have some ideas that definitely tie into your long-range plans." The note had everything—familiarity, evidence that Webster was listening, and the thought that Webster felt so strongly about the client that he was already thinking of approaches that could be used.

Webster added another touch to his note; it was handwritten, not typed or printed from a word processor. He used 4" X 5" stationery (so the note stood out from the recipient's other letters), and he put a stamp on it instead of running it through the company's postage meter machine. (To this day, Webster writes his own thank-you notes, all by hand.)

Thank-you notes have, of course, become standard in business, but not handwritten ones. Also, 4" X 5" notes are not standard. When they are received, they have a psychological impact. The recipient looks at the note and realizes that the writer took time to put it together. It was not dictated or written by a secretary. It has impact.

How a thank-you note should be phrased depends on what the writer is trying to accomplish. For example, a businessperson (or anyone) who was invited to dinner, might put something together like the following to the hostess:

> You were very generous to include me in that lovely dinner
> on Friday, and I am extremely grateful.

Notice the language, which is geared (with words such as lovely and generous) to appeal to a female. Suppose the dinner was at a restaurant and the host was a businessman? The note might be rephrased and would say:

> It was extremely kind of you to include [or *invite*] me to
> dinner last Friday, and I am very grateful for the invitation.

> The company was superb and the food was marvelous. I
> particularly enjoyed meeting [*name*] and being able to
> reminisce about some enjoyable times.

Both notes exude warmth and sincerity, the two elements every thank-you note should have.

Although Webster's note was not thanking someone for dinner, it still exuded friendliness and familiarity. Eventually, Webster won the client, and he gives much of the credit to the simple thank-you note he took time to write . . . by hand.

HIDDEN MEANINGS

Webster's note did the two key things that all letters and memos should accomplish: it (1) communicated a message and (2) projected an image. Every letter and memo communicates, but the message may be fuzzy or inaccurate, or the image may be wrong. Take, for instance, the following memo from the senior vice president of a large insurance company. It went to every employee at the firm's corporate office.

> It has come to my attention that last night, a [*item*] was
> stolen from [*name*]'s desk. It is obvious that the person who

took the [*item*] had a key and access to this floor, which means that it was one of our employees. I would like to remind everyone to keep their desks locked and remove all valuables every evening. Should someone be apprehended for the theft, it will result in immediate dismissal.

The memo did nothing to endear the vice president (and the company) to the employees. It also suffers from one of the great sins of letter writing—negativity. And it reveals another fault of letter writing: being hasty. The vice president was obviously upset and wrote the memo before thinking about it. If she had waited, thought about it and the consequences of using the language she chose, she would certainly have revised it.

Certainly, no firm wants to tolerate theft, but there are other ways of "laying down the law." In this situation, the vice president was upset at the theft, but she wrote a hasty memo in which she assumed that one of the employees was the thief. This may have been true; however, without proof, it was a mistake to make accusations. The memo was extremely formal, which further strained the relationships between the company and the employees. If the executive had held the memo for a day, or even a few hours, she might have revised the language and kept the goodwill and cooperation of the company's employees, instead of alienating (and insulting) most. It would have said,

This morning we learned that a [*item*] was missing from [*name*]'s desk. Obviously, this is a valuable piece of equipment which we do not want to lose, and we have already started an investigation into the incident. If anyone has information as to what might have happened to it, please see me.

Until we determine what did happen, I would like to remind everyone to keep office doors and desks locked. Please follow personnel procedures and make sure all confidential data is securely stored before leaving for the evening.

While in-person meetings have the advantage of offsetting any misunderstanding through facial expressions and body language, letters and memos do not. Every word has a meaning, and some words denote more than one definition, as well as hidden meanings. The good letter and memo writer keeps this in mind. Letters and memos are not written to an object, but to a living, breathing person. Smart writers outline correspondence, make rough drafts, and then put themselves in the place of the recipient before it is ever sent. They ask, "Does it make sense? Does it say what I want? Does it get the message across? Does it have the correct tone (language)? Style? Is there language in it that may be misunderstood? Is it written with multisyllable, abstract words, or is it straightforward, easy to understand, and dominated by one-syllable words?"

SIX FORMS OF LETTERS

All letters generally fall into one of six forms:

1. Sales, which includes fundraising and similar correspondence
2. Thank you or other goodwill notes
3. Congratulations
4. Apology
5. Collection
6. Condolence/sympathy

These six forms can be further divided into two additional categories:

1. Formal
2. Informal

Memos can be categorized, too:

1. Personnel announcement, including policies and procedures
2. Thanks and congratulations
3. Reminders, requests, business recaps

Characteristics of informal correspondence are contractions, the dominance of one-syllable words, and the use of adjectives that convey a sense of intimacy. For example, *lovely*, *delightful*, and *exciting* are typical of letters and memos that bring the writer closer to the reader.

TONE AND STYLE

Adjectives and adverbs, the qualifiers and descriptive words in the English language, create the tone and style of letters and memos. *Tone* is communicated by the choice of words and how the language is used to convey an emotional feeling or tonality. For example, tone can be objective, subjective, or emotional. The memo that berated employees for the theft was subjective and emotional. In contrast, the story on page one of the daily newspaper is usually objective and contains few emotionally-charged words—just the facts. Many business letters are written this way, too.

Style adds further dimensions of language to the tone of the correspondence, highlighting its degree of formality versus familiarity.

Take, for instance, the following two sales memos, which were written by a pair of sales managers in the Midwest. Both, incidentally worked for the same company, although they handled different product lines. Notice the familiarity of the first. The style is informal, the language familiar, the words primarily monosyllables. This memo got the message across. It also lets the salespeople know that the sales manager is behind them.

> Yesterday, I met with [*name*] and we went through some of the sales problems we have encountered during the past nine months. We are off 14% compared to last year and [*name*] is getting pressure from the Board to pull out all stops in order to make up the deficit during the last quarter. I know some of you have ideas as to what we might be able to do to make up the decrease. During the next week, I will be talking to each of you via telephone, for an exchange of ideas. We may also hold a regional sales meeting to kick off the fourth quarter. Before calling, I would like each of you to obtain input from the field to see what suggestions they might have. We are all in this together and, hopefully, if we put our heads together we can come up with a campaign that will not only enable us to make up the 14% but go far beyond it.

Contrast this with the second memo, which has unpleasant connotations throughout. Both sales managers needed improved performance. However, the former got the sense of urgency across without threats or alienating any salespeople. The latter, incidentally, caused several top salespeople to look elsewhere for employment. Employees may respond to threats in the short run, but in the long run, memos that have veiled threats do little for morale or for long-range performance.

> We are entering the last quarter of the year, and performance has been down 14% in comparison to last year. Yesterday, I met with [*name*] and he told me that unless sales are made up in this last quarter, we can look forward to cuts in the first quarter of next year. That also means merit increases and commission draws will not be forthcoming. I will be calling regional managers in the next week to obtain a forecast of sales for the last quarter.

The first of the two memos is going to do more to foster teamwork and has a better chance of motivating salespeople through cooperation. Today, as always, good salespeople are hard to find, and trying to get the most out of them through threats never works. It almost always ends in the company losing the top producers and retaining those on the bottom rung.

SALES LETTERS AND GOODWILL NOTES

Of all letters and memos, those dealing with sales are perhaps the most important and the easiest to foul up. The following are a selection that fit numerous sales situations and can be used for almost any industry.

Postpurchase selling is critical to the survival of most businesses. To prosper, businesspeople should maintain a constant flow of communication with customers. Letter 1–4 is an example of the type of letter that is frequently sent to previous customers. There are numerous variations of this, and the items can be substituted with services. The postscript (P.S.) serves to emphasize a point that the letter writer does not want the reader to miss.

The short introductory note in Letter 1–5 has an important close: "I'll be in your area next [*day*] and will call." This leaves it up to the salesperson to be the aggressor, not the prospect. The most successful salespeople use this approach. Never leave it to the customer to make the call.

Letter 1–6 was written by a loan officer in the Northeast. His track record is exceptional and shows that even in the finance industry, well-

Dear   :

   Our records indicate that two years ago, your purchased a
[*item*] for your son [*daughter*], [*name*], for his [*her*] birthday,
which falls on [*date*].

   With his [*her*] birthday coming up again, you may wish to
surprise him [*her*] with one of the beautiful, new models we
have available in our shop.

   Incidentally, we offer a trade-in allowance and, of course,
would be happy to store the [*item*] in order to keep it "under
wraps" until that special day.

   Give it some thought, and if you feel that [*name*] would be
pleased, come in to visit us at your convenience, and we will
show you our stock.

   If, instead, you are looking for an alternative gift, we have a
selection of alternatives as well. Give me a call, and I would be
happy to go through some of the new items that might be of
interest to your son [*daughter*]. I look forward to hearing from
you.

                    Sincerely,

                    [*Name*]

P.S. For previous customers, a special (– _____ %) discount is in
effect for the next 30 days.

Letter 1–4: A postpurchase sales letter.

Dear   :

    Our firm supplies products and programs that are designed for schools. We have enclosed a brochure that shows the types of programs we have put together—programs that will generate funds for your school while exposing your students to the experience of selling products.

    These programs have been successfully tested in over 1000 public and private schools throughout the country. Without exception, both schools and students have benefited.

    If you are interested in having students participate in any of our programs, I would be happy to discuss them with you. I'll be in your area next [*day*] and will call beforehand to see whether we can get together.

Letter 1–5: A letter of introduction with a key final sentence.

Dear   :

    If you are like many of our customers, you have probably held off from borrowing funds during the past year because interest rates were high.

    Now, however, rates have come down to a reasonable level and you may wish to consider the advantages of having one loan with one payment versus many loans with a multitude of payments.

    Consolidation has advantages. We'd like to visit with you to explain those advantages, explore your financial situation, and see whether we can be of service.

    I'll give you a call to see if we might arrange a mutually convenient time.

Letter 1–6: An aggressive, and effective, introductory letter from a real estate loan officer.

constructed letters and an aggressive sales posture help firms to prosper. A variation of this letter has the interest rates inserted; however, the rates are only used when they are extremely low.

Letter 1–7 welcomes a new tenant. A note of appreciation shows a nice touch that few landlords think about. It can often lead to more cooperative tenants and favorable word-of-mouth advertising, which certainly helps in a market where an abundance of rental units is available. This same note, with variations, can be used by vendors who are trying to sell products to new renters or buyers (as in Letters 1–8 and 1–9).

In Letters 1–8 and 1–9 newcomers are welcomed to the neighborhood by a vendor, and in an effort to get them to drop in, a special discount is enclosed.

Though it's important to make new customers feel welcome, it's *crucial* to keep existing customers happy. Preferred customer sales are not a new way of pleasing customers—they are advertised all the time. However, Letter 1–10 highlights the value of a handwritten note, which is seldom sent, but which has considerable impact.

Letters 1–11 and 1–12 are similar, but 1–12 can be used for service businesses or for letters from manufacturers to representatives or distributors. Notice, too, that Letter 1–12 puts the burden of contact on the salesperson—which it should.

Any local service business or manufacturing concern can also adapt the approach in Letter 1–13. When customers have not been around, a handwritten note can be especially effective.

The simple thank you note in Letter 1–14 can be handwritten, too. It not only thanks the account for the time they took, but it also serves to reinforce the introduction of a new salesperson. The last line can be varied to make the note even more personal. For example, if the customer talked about his son, daughter, or something else, the line could be rewritten to reflect it:

I enjoyed hearing about your son's achievements and can understand why you are so proud of him.

That line would be followed by "The hospitality you showed me yesterday."

It is always difficult introducing someone new to accounts. In this type of letter, adjectives can help significantly. Notice the line in Letter 1–15 that says "He has some fascinating thoughts," which also helps open the door because it will usually pique the curiosity of the client, who would like to know what the salesperson knows.

Dear   :

It is my pleasure to welcome you to your new home.

As tenants, I hope that you will avail yourselves of the amenities that are offered, including the swimming pool, sauna room, gymnasium, and tennis court.

I do request, however, that any guests you may have visiting use our guest parking area in order to avoid any inconvenience to other tenants.

Thank you for selecting [*name of apartment*], and I sincerely hope you find your new home comfortable and enjoyable. If I can be of any assistance, please let me know.

Letter 1–7: A letter welcoming a tenant can promote good will and generate future business.

Dear   :

Welcome to the city of [*name*]. We know that you will enjoy living here and we're pleased that you've selected this community to be your new home.

[*Name of firm*] has been here since [*year*] and carries a complete line of the finest brand names of appliances available. We also offer rebuilt and used models, which are sold with our personal warranty. Incidentally, we also accept your older appliances as a trade-in if you decide to purchase a new one from us. Should you require service on one of your appliances that is no longer under warranty our service department will make the necessary repairs and, in addition, we will provide you with a one year guarantee on all parts replaced.

If I can answer any question about our firm or the community, please call. And as a special welcome, I've enclosed a certificate which entitles you to a (– _____ %) discount on any new or used appliance.

I look forward to meeting you.

Letter 1–8: A letter to a new tenant or homeowner from a local retailer.

Dear   :

As a way of saying "welcome" to [*city*], we have enclosed a gift certificate that entitles you to (– _____ %) off the regular price of having your carpets and upholstery cleaned.

Our company is fully equipped to shampoo or steam clean, deodorize, and Scotchguard® your carpets while giving attention to any trouble spots and protecting your carpet and furniture during this service.

Most important, we have been providing service to this community for _____ years and we hope that you will give us the opportunity to show you the fine work we do and the expertise of our bonded service personnel.

Letter 1–9: A letter to a new tenant or homeowner from a local service.

Dear   :

We missed you!
We didn't see you at our Summer Sale, nor did we see you at our Fall Sale. After putting our heads together, we concluded that one possible reason for your having stayed away so long might be that you don't like crowds. So, we came up with the following solution:

A PRE-[name] SALE

OPEN ONLY TO PREFERRED CUSTOMERS

DECEMBER 12, 1987

5:00 P.M.–9:00 P.M.

We look forward to seeing you!

Letter 1–10: A preferred customer sales note.

Dear   :

    It has been more than six months since you came to visit us, and we've missed you.

    If you have a chance, please stop in to see us. I think you will be surprised by some of the new merchandise we have available. As one of our preferred customers, you will, of course, be entitled to use your ten percent (10%), lifetime discount privilege.

    I look forward to seeing you.

Letter 1–11: A follow-up letter from a retailer.

Dear   :

It has been quite a while since we had the opportunity to be of service to you.

We have introduced many new innovations into our product line—innovations that I feel certain would be of interest to your company. I'll call to see if we might get together to show you some of them.

In the meantime, thank you for your time and consideration.

Sincerely,

Letter 1–12: A follow-up letter that can be used by a service or manufacturer.

Dear   :

    It has been more than six months since we have had the opportunity to service your automobile, and we've missed you.

    So, we are inviting you to bring your [*make of car*] into our shop for a free inspection and tune-up. We advocate periodic inspection of vehicles as a means for assuring safety and for preventing major repairs by detecting problems early.

    We hope that you will accept our offer. We have set aside the hours between 8:00 A.M. and 1:00 P.M., Monday through Friday for your convenience. An appointment is not necessary.

Letter 1–13: A follow-up letter from an automobile service center.

Dear   :

Thank you for affording me the opportunity to meet with you and members of your staff yesterday afternoon.

I know that [*name*] serviced your account for many years and made many friends at your firm. While his presence will be missed, I can assure you that you will continue to receive the fine service that has always been [*name of company*]'s trademark.

The hospitality you showed me yesterday explains why [*name*] held your organization in such high regard.

Letter 1–14: A thank you note from a new salesperson.

Dear   :

   It is my great pleasure to advise you that [*name*] is now representing our firm in your area.

   [*Name*] has been handling our accounts in [*city*] for some time and is extremely knowledgable. He's [*she's*] been in our business for _____ years. He [*she*] also has some fascinating thoughts on the business in your area.

   [*Name*] will be in your area on [*date*] in the morning and would like to schedule an appointment at that time.

   We'll call to see whether this date is convenient.

Letter 1–15: A letter introducing a new salesperson.

Letter 1–16, however, is far less successful. The introduction should be stronger and the firm should be calling the client to definitely confirm the time. There is nothing more difficult for a new salesperson than walking into a client's place of business and not being expected.

Letter 1–17 is a revised version and shows what should be done with introductory letters.

Letter 1–18 illustrates a nice welcome letter from a small, West Coast bank that has managed to make money for 18 consecutive years regardless of economic conditions. Bankers often forget that present depositors are the greatest source of new business. Consequently, a well-thought-out letter-writing program is of paramount importance to those in the industry. Each letter that follows the introductory note should discuss a "product" that will benefit the depositor.

Special time-limited previews convey a sense of urgency to customers (Letter 1–19). It gives the line more importance and sets it apart from others. Time-limited previews are always better than two- or three-day open houses.

The holidays give businesspeople a chance to say thanks to customers without trying to sell them something. Once again, thank-you notes such as Letter 1–20 should be handwritten.

Letter 1–21 is from a Southern manufacturer, who has received excellent response to it. Although everyone says the best time to take advantage of low prices is now, this manufacturer actually gives his customers a reason. The rationale makes the claim more credible.

One of the toughest businesses to make successful is a restaurant. The owner of a small French restaurant in the Midwest always makes it a point to get the name and address of first-time customers and to write them a note (Letter 1–22).

Letter 1–23 was handwritten. The author, a Southern travel agent, wants feedback, but more than that, she looks for contact with the prospect.

The West Coast software manufacturer who authored Letter 1–24 gets hundreds of inquiries each week. In addition to sending a brochure in response to the inquiry, he always mentions an "innovation" that will be introduced shortly. This is the kind of line that prompts telephone calls and opens the door for a sales call. Computer people certainly cannot afford to be left behind.

Letter 1–25 illustrates a similar approach. The third paragraph does two things: (1) it sparks the interest of the customer, and (2) it gives the company a reason to call on the prospect the following month.

Dear   :

We have assigned [*name*] as our new representative for your area. [*Name*] has been with our firm for some time and is extremely experienced in all aspects of the industry.

[*Name*] will be coming to [*city*] on [*date*] and would like to call on you in the morning. If there is any problem with the date or time, please let us know.

Letter 1–16: A weak letter of introduction.

Dear   :

    We have assigned [*name*] as our new representative for your area. [*Name*] has been with us for _____ years and is noted for his [*her*] experience in the industry.

    [*Name*] will be coming to [*city*] on [*date*] and would like to call on you in the morning, if that is convenient. I'll give you a call to confirm the time. I think you'll find [*name*] fascinating and an excellent source of information on what's happening in the business.

Letter 1–17: A revision of Letter 1–16 that has a stronger presentation and includes reference to a follow-up call by the firm to confirm the appointment.

Dear   :

I would like to take this opportunity to personally thank you for choosing our bank to handle your account. I know a great amount of care goes into choosing a banker, and your decision reaffirms my belief in the old-fashioned ways of banking. We believe that our depositors enjoy the personal contact they receive at each one of our branches.

We employ the latest technology in computers, but we will never abandon our personal commitment to you, the customer—our greatest asset.

We feel strongly committed to personal banking and to personal relationships.

I hope you will feel free to use any of the many services we have designed to make your banking experience as enjoyable and comprehensive as possible.

Letter 1–18: A thank you letter from a bank emphasizing its commitment to personal service.

Dear   :

We are pleased to announce that our new product line is ready to be shown.

I'm confident that you will be delightfully surprised when you see our latest innovations. We are holding a special preview on [*date*] from [*hours*] and would like to invite you to visit our display room.

I'm sure you'll find that the new line is well worth the visit.

Letter 1–19: A letter announcing a time-limited preview of a new product line.

Dear   :

   The holiday season offers me a chance to extend my personal thanks to our special friends, and to offer our best wishes for the future.
   We take pride in our business, and customers like you make going to work each day a rewarding experience.
   All of us wish you a very merry Christmas and a Happy New Year. We tip our glasses to you. Thanks again for a wonderful year.

Letter 1–20: A holiday greeting to clients is always appropriate.

Dear   :

    The best time to take advantage of our low prices is now!

    Why? According to the Department of Commerce, interest rates are slated to go up 1% during the next four months!

    So, why not beat inflation and drop by soon? We are having a special Preferred Customer Sale, and I'm sure you will be pleased with the products and prices. In any event, drop by and say "hello."

Letter 1–21: A sales letter that reinforces its point with statistics.

Dear   :

It was my pleasure to serve you and your guests for [*lunch/ dinner*] at our restaurant on [*date*].

I hope the cuisine and service were beyond your expectations. We always strive to maintain our high standards.

Thank you for the opportunity to serve you.

Sincerely,

Letter 1–22: A thank you note from a restaurant owner.

Dear   :

    Thank you for giving us the opportunity to make the travel arrangements for your recent trip.

    I hope that the trip was successful and the travel and accommodations everything you wanted. If you have a chance, I would appreciate hearing any thoughts or comments you might have on the arrangements.

    Once again, our thanks.

Letter 1–23: A thank you note from a travel agent.

Dear   :

Thank you for your recent inquiry into the software packages we currently have on the market.

We are enclosing a brochure and would like to point out that our software is compatible with almost all of the major hardware available in the United States. We are also preparing a new package that will be introduced shortly. It will be quite revolutionary, yet extremely easy to use.

If you have any specific questions, please call me at [*telephone*], or just drop a line. I look forward to hearing from you.

Letter 1–24: A thank you letter from a computer software manufacturer that prompts calls with hints about a new innovation.

Dear   :

    Your letter regarding our product line has been brought to my attention, and I would like to thank you for your interest in [*firm's name*].

    I have enclosed a price list and a catalogue that describes our full line of products. These should help to familiarize you with the high quality of our family of goods.

    The one item we have not included is our new [*item*], which will be ready next month. It is going to be quite a revolutionary package for the industry, and I'll send you updated information as soon as it is ready.

    If you have any questions about our products, prices, or policies, please call.

    Thank you again for your interest.

Letter 1–25: Similar to Letter 1–24, this can be used by any manufacturer and additionally sets up further correspondence.

CHAPTER **2**

The Magic Words

Numerous professions have stereotype reputations.
Through the use of magic words, negative images can
be made positive for virtually any professional.

First came the request:

> Dear   :
>
> I need your help—more specifically, is it possible that I can
> get an extension on the existing loan I have with the bank
> for a period of six months?
>
> Naturally, if I can have the extension, I would pay whatever
> prevailing rates the bank charges.

Then, the short, to-the-point answer from the well-known West
Coast banker:

> Dear   :
>
> Your pleas for fiscal aid did not fall on deaf ears. Within this
> tabernacle of fiscal integrity beats a heart as "big as all
> outdoors." I am therefore, empowered to grant your request
> and to this end enclose documents pertinent to successful
> conclusion of your wish.
>
> Your Humble Servant,

The first letter is quite familiar. Similar prose has crossed the desks of
thousands of bankers. The answer, of course, is either going to be yes
or no, but how that answer is conveyed can paint an image in the
borrower's mind of the banker as well as of the bank. The brief and
specific answer also provided a few laughs for the borrower and left
him with a positive, upbeat image of the bank and its management.
The reply is one that would work between any banker and borrower
who know each other.

USING DESCRIPTIVE TERMS

What makes the banker's letter effective is the language . . . or the "magic words." Some words sell better than others. Some grab, while others fall short. Magic words are ordinary words, words we are used to seeing and hearing; but they are made magic by their placement in letters and memos. They are placed in an unexpected context. For instance, a banker would not be expected to use words such as "fiscal integrity," "empowered," "wish," and "your humble servant" in answering a loan request.

Using words in unusual contexts creates intriguing, fascinating prose. The most effective words for this purpose are descriptive and almost always have more connotative meaning than the literal dictionary definition.

It does not take a professional writer to create letters and memos with magic words. In fact, businesspeople can master the art with little trouble. Step one is to create the basic message. Take, for instance, the following thank-you memo, which was sent from a CEO to his vice president following a speech that the vice president had helped him to prepare. Initially, the CEO created the basic message:

Dear   :

The speech went well, and I wanted to thank you for your help.

When he went through and inserted suitable descriptive words wherever he could:

Dear   :

Thank you for your *admirable* help in connection with the speech I gave the other day. It went *extremely* well, and there has been *considerable* comment—all *favorable*.

With the addition of four words, the memo has greater meaning and more impact. There is more warmth and punch. All businesspeople can do the same. Initially, they create the message, then they go back through and add magic words (adjectives and adverbs) to give the letter or memo more impact.

The addition of magic words works with all correspondence. For example, the following memo was sent to a secretary from a department supervisor.

Dear   :

On behalf of [*company*], I would like to thank you for the time and effort you put into our opening. You helped make the day successful and our kickoff a success.

The supervisor went through the note and marked the areas where adjectives (or adverbs) would fit. Almost always, they can be inserted before nouns or before other adjectives.

Dear   :

On behalf of [*company*], I would like to extend the company's *heartfelt* thanks for the time and *extraordinary* effort you put in to help make our opening day a *roaring* success. You *certainly* helped make the kickoff *truly* *remarkable*.

IMPORTANCE OF THE WORD GUARANTEE

All any businessperson needs to put together letters and memos with magic words is a dictionary and a thesaurus. With them, you can find a host of words that give letters and memos punch. For example, here are just a few of the hundreds of possibilities:

amazing	premier
dramatic	prominent
electrifying	seductive
engrossing	significant
entertaining	sizzling
esteemed	spellbinding
extraordinary	spicy
fetching	stirring
imaginative	stunning
knockout	tantalizing
landmark	unforgettable
lovely	vibrant
mesmerizing	winsome
noteworthy	world-class

No discussion of words would be complete without the one word that means more to customers than anything: *guarantee*. Whether it is "unconditional" or only "30-day," *guarantee* says that the company stands behind the product. The word adds credibility to any letter that is exchanged between business and customer, and it should be used whenever possible.

BEFORE AND AFTER—WHAT IT LOOKS LIKE

By themselves, magic words to not have as much impact as they do when used in an appropriate context. When they are used properly, however, they can make a significant difference in a letter. For example:

Before	After
It was a good speech	It was an extraordinary address
An excellent version	A stirring rendition
A good performance	An engrossing performance
A perfect presentation	An unforgettable presentation

In actual correspondence, the words have even greater impact. A New York designer drafted the following, which he was going to send to a style writer on a local newspaper.

Dear . . . .:

My 19__ designs are ready for your perusal!

My associates say they are some of the best they have ever seen, this year or any.

My partner agrees, and I think you will, too.

Though short and to the point, it does little to motivate the recipient. The designer examined the letter and revised it, using words with impact; that is, magic words.

My 19__ designs are ready for your perusal!

My associates say they are lovely and fetching (aren't all designs?), yet these have one other attribute . . . they are unforgettable.

I prefer my partner's comment—"They will set the fashion world on its collective ears." They are bold, original, and fascinating.

I think you will agree.

Or, take this letter, which was sent from a realtor to a prospect.

Dear   :

I think we have found the home you have been searching for.

It has the amenities we discussed, is located in the area we pinpointed, and is available at the right price.

I'm planning to see it first-hand next Saturday. Would you be available to come along?

Before the realtor mailed it, she made several revisions:

Dear   :

We've found that breathtaking home . . .

It has an incredibly dramatic view, a superb location, the grounds are overwhelming, . . . and the price is right!

I'm planning to tour it again this Saturday . . . can you come?

INDUSTRY TERMINOLOGY

Every industry, profession, and business has its own magic words. The following was sent by an East Coast (not IBM) computer salesperson to a prospect:

Dear   :

The most talked-about new computer in the business, a computer that has won *accolades* from every critic in the business, is about to be honored by _____ *Magazine* as the "most *noteworthy* data processing innovation" in a decade . . . and it isn't even on the market.

I thought you would like to get an *advance* preview of this *sensational* piece of equipment. I'll have a prototype model next week and will give you a call to see if you can set aside some time for a *preview* look at this *celebrated entrant* into the data processing field.

In the entertainment business, dramatic descriptions are particularly important. The following was sent by a performer who was mentioned several times in a column written by a local writer.

> I have just read your column, and I was *flattered* by your *kind* references to me and the way you recalled the *marvelous* incident.

Contrast it with:

> I have just read your column and appreciate the references to me and the way you recalled the incident.

Flattered and *marvelous* have substantial additional meaning. Contrast *flattered* with *appreciate*, which is overused and has lost meaning, and you can see what a difference just one word can make.

Thousands of firms count on the mails for business. Typically, a prospect who sends for a catalog gets something similar to the following back in the mail. The following two letters were both sent by mail-order catalog firms that market products to dentists.

> Thank you for your inquiry about our _____ equipment.
>
> Our enclosed catalog will give you all the background information about the _____.
>
> If there is anything else we can tell you, please call.

A typical, mail-order catalog cover letter—certainly without anything memorable about it. Now, look at the approach of this firm's competition.

> We were pleased to receive in today's mail your inquiry about our _____. Without question, the inquiry indicates the intelligent and sensible approach you are taking to your entry into the profession.
>
> Obviously, you will be the one to use the equipment. Therefore, it is up to you to examine, scrutinize, and judge it on its own merits before making a decision.
>
> Our catalog will familiarize you with much of the pertinent background information needed in order to make a wise choice on this essential equipment.

Thank you for your letter and your kind consideration. I know that our equipment will meet your diverse needs. However, if there is any question I can answer, please call me at the toll-free number below:

[*phone number*]

My sincere best wishes in the years ahead for a rewarding and distinguished practice.

Both letters were generated on word processors, but the latter is loaded with magic (descriptive) words. There is no question as to which is more effective. One letter is matter-of-fact and to the point. The other conveys to the recipient a feeling that this firm wants to do more than sell equipment; it also cares about the dentist and her new practice.

THE SCIENCE OF LETTERS AND MEMOS

Cecil Wharton (not his real last name) owns a small, but rapidly growing, cosmetics company in the Southwestern United States. Wharton started as a door-to-door salesman for a rival company and learned how powerful words could be in person. When he launched his company 15 years ago, he knew there was no way he could personally see every one of his customers. He realized that correspondence was critical to his success because he could not possibly visit all the manufacturing representatives and customers who were selling his line. That's when he decided to make a science out of letter and memo writing. He began to compile and classify words that he knew would be appropriate for his industry.

Wharton says, "It is important for executives—or anyone for that matter—to understand that what we put on paper presents an image of us and of our company. Put the wrong word down and you can kill a sale or ruin the morale of an employee. In my business, letter and memo writing is as important as pricing."

To inspire employees, Wharton has created a series of internal memos relating to production, each of which can be altered and used in any industry.

I would like to *personally* thank each and every one of you for the *magnificent* effort you put in during the past few *hectic* weeks. We all know how busy we are this time of the year and how *critical* your performance is to the *well-being* of the company. Once again, you all did a *sensational* job and the production output was *overwhelming*.

Note the italicized words and the impact they give to the memo. All are descriptive terms not normally found in a production environment. When they are used, they have enormous impact.

Our season is here. During the coming weeks all of us will have a *staggering* work load and each one of you will be a *vital link* to our success. As always, I am counting on you to put everything aside and do your usual *sensational* job. If you have any suggestions don't hold back—we need them. Here's to an *exhilarating* and *challenging* two months and the future of the company!

Wharton does not just ask his employees to work hard, he asks them to join him and emphasizes how important their performance is to the well-being of the company. Similarly, any firms that have heavy seasonal demands can inspire teamwork and superlative efforts as Wharton does each year, simply by involving employees and telling them they are needed.

Wharton inspires customers, too. He has developed a series of letters that can be adapted by those in other industries and professions. Letter 2–1 is one that Wharton sends to newly opened accounts. It welcomes the client, compliments the firm for its reputation, and sets forth credit terms. Note the magic words and how they are used.

COLLECTION LETTERS

One of the most difficult pieces of correspondence to write is the collection, or overdue account, note. Wharton put together the note on page 66, which he sends to accounts that have not responded to normal terms, and that have not talked to Wharton's credit department, to give them either a reason for the lateness or a new date for payment. The tone of Wharton's note differs from most collection letters. Wharton observes, "It makes the debtor feel obligated. Remember, in most cases he has been screamed at by everyone. Suddenly, he gets a letter from me that does not scream but offers some consolation. In more than 90% of the cases, our funds are paid within two weeks after this letter is received, or the debtor calls me and arranges a payout schedule."

Dear   :

Thank you for opening an account with our company. As one of the leaders in this industry, I can assure you that our products and our services will not disappoint you.

Your firm's noteworthy reputation is well-known, and we are proud to have the opportunity to serve such a prominent company.

I would like to take this opportunity to briefly set forth our terms and conditions for maintaining an open account with our company. Invoices are payable within 30 days of receipt, with a 2% discount available if your payment is remitted within ten (10) days of receipt. We consider this incentive an excellent opportunity for our customers to increase their profit margin.

Letter 2–1: A welcome letter with a nice use of magic words.

Dear   :

It happens to all of us . . . we forget and it is understandable.

We live in a fast-paced world and, at times, our bills and obligations take a back seat to some other problems. I know that is what probably happened in your firm's case.

Our accounting department told me you were overdue on two of your invoices. I asked them not to send one of their standard "overdue notices" since your firm has been a long-time customer and we have known each other for years. I insisted that if any letters were going to be sent about past due bills, they would come from me, to you, as friends.

We've built a good relationship between our firms and I want to keep it. Would you give me a call this week so we can discuss the account and any problems you might be having.

Notice, too, the subtle deadline that is mentioned in the note. The debtor is asked to call this week. Whenever possible, deadlines should be put in correspondence, especially credit or collection notices. Without a deadline, the recipient has an out and can further delay payment.

LETTERS FROM NONPROFIT ORGANIZATIONS

Nonprofit organizations, as well as profit-making ones, need to use magic words and phrases suitable for each situation. Letters 2–2 through 2–8 cover a wide range of circumstances, from congratulatory notes to thank-you notes. Each letter uses magic words to make it more effective.

Congratulations

Letters 2–2 through 2–4 show several congratulatory notes and suggest ways in which they can subtly reinforce participants' decisions to become involved in community nonprofit organizations.

Dear   :

    Congratulations on your induction into [*the organization, e.g., Rotary Club*]. Welcome to our community.

    Please contact me if our [*name of organization*] can help you and your family as they settle into our area.

                  Kindest regards,

Letter 2–2: A welcome-to-the-community letter from an organization such as the Rotary Club.

Dear   :

      Congratulations on your election to our Board of Managers. We greatly appreciate your acceptance of a position as a member of this body. I believe that you'll find your participation to be challenging, stimulating, and rewarding.

      Because you have indicated an interest in serving on our Budget and Finance Committee, I want to invite you to our next meeting, scheduled for [*date and time*], in the conference room at the [*place of meeting*]. A copy of this committee's Commission and its Chart of Work for the coming year is enclosed for your review.

      Please put this meeting on your calendar, and plan to attend. I look forward both to seeing you on [*date*] and to working with you as we make [*the organization*] the best it can be.

Letter 2–3: A letter of congratulations to a newly elected member of an organization's Board of Managers.

Dear   :

 This note just offers a word of thanks for your agreeing to help with our annual support campaign. I believe that you'll enjoy the experience, and, as you know, your work will greatly benefit [*name of organization*].

 I look forward to seeing you soon at one of our report meetings.

Letter 2–4: A letter of thanks for volunteering help in a support campaign.

Dear   :

We wish to thank you and [*company*] for the tremendous gift
in support of [*organization*]. Your help goes a long way in
allowing us to continue and expand programs and services that
make our community a good place in which to live and work.
You have my pledge that your contribution will be used wisely to
this end.

In addition, I will see to it that [*company*] receives all
appropriate recognition and that the company's exemplary
community citizenship is fully appreciated by those who benefit
from it. You will be receiving information from us on an
ongoing basis in regard to our progress and the impact that
your gift is having on the lives of those we serve.

Letter 2–5: A letter of thanks acknowledging a monetary gift.

Dear   :

It was great to hear that [*company*] is providing a [*amount*] gift to sponsor this year's [*name of program*]. I know that this gift results in no small measure from your work with [*name of organization*], and [*company*]'s desire to support that work. We are grateful to both you and [*company*] for what you do to help our program.

I will see to it that you both continue to receive the recognition you deserve. On behalf of all those who benefit from your efforts, please accept our gratitude.

Letter 2–6: A letter of thanks acknowledging a monetary gift to a specific program.

Dear   :

   Thank you for your recent donation of [*item*] for [*name of organization*].

   The generosity of contributors like you enables [*organization*] to continue its programs of service to [*youth and others*] in the community.

   Again, our sincere thanks.

Letter 2–7: A letter of thanks for contributing a specific item.

Dear   :

This note expresses our appreciation for your generosity in providing door prizes for this year's support campaign. These prizes arc exceedingly important in providing a motivational climate for our campaign.

Your thoughtfulness certainly helped contribute to the success of an extraordinary campaign, and for that we are very grateful.

Letter 2–8: A letter thanking a company for items used in fundraising.

Notes of Appreciation

Gifts—financial or otherwise—should always be acknowledged. The thank-you notes in Letters 2–5 and 2–6 suggest an excellent format for nonprofit organizations to follow when gifts of money are donated.

In addition, it's important for organizations to write notes of appreciation for donations of objects for use by the organization (e.g., 2–7) or for use in fund-raising (e.g., 2–8).

As Letters 2–9 and 2–10 show, appreciation should also be affirmed for services and resources made available to nonprofit organizations.

Finally, and perhaps most importantly, it is essential for nonprofit organizations to acknowledge the tremendous value of community leaders, volunteers, and others who support organizations with their time, energy, and dedication (Letters 2–11 through 2–14).

Letter 2–15 shows how a business might respond to an award or certificate of appreciation. When a supportive member of the community leaves the area, a letter such as 2–16 might be written.

Difficult Letters

Letters of appreciation are among the most gratifying anyone may write. At the other end of the spectrum are letters requesting that a donor complete payment for money that was pledged but not yet delivered. Letter 2–17 offers an example of how such a difficult letter may be worded.

Equally as difficult to write is a letter apologizing for a mistake. Letter 2–18 may suggest one way in which this situation may be handled.

APOLOGY LETTERS

Nonprofit organizations are not the only ones needing to make written apologies. For-profit businesses encounter a wide variety of situations in which apologies are necessary. For example, answering complaints can be difficult. Letter 2–19 not only offers an apology but also offers the consumer something to placate her or him. When companies can offer something to make up for the mistake, the letter becomes more potent.

Dear   :

Thanks for your tremendous help and cooperation in allowing [*organization name*] to park its buses in one of your parking lots off of 190th street. As you know, we have had substantial difficulty in finding an area to secure these vehicles at night.

Your community-mindedness and willingness to help with this problem is greatly appreciated, as is your company's efforts to work with kids over the summer months.

Letter 2–9: A letter thanking a company for the use of its facilities.

Dear   :

I greatly enjoyed getting together with you for lunch the other day. We appreciate the support that you and [*the hospital*] give to our [*name of organization*]. We look forward to the prospect of further developing that relationship in order to meet the needs of the people that live and work in our area.

We wish you the best with your upcoming campaign and look forward to seeing you again.

Letter 2–10: A letter thanking a company for hospital services.

Dear   :

   I've been sitting here trying to think of an appropriate superlative to express my appreciation for your leadership and accomplishments in chairing this year's campaign. Though I've been unable to find a superlative that is adequate to express my feelings for your leadership, "superterrific" comes as close as anything I can think of.

   I very much enjoyed working with you, learning from you, and sharing the success of our magnificent accomplishment with you. You certainly deserve all the accolades that have come your way. I, for one, am awed by the results of our efforts.

   [*Name*], thank you again for your help. I am grateful for the time and the talent that you gave to this year's effort, and I look forward to our continuing work together.

Letter 2–11: A thank you letter to the chairperson of a campaign.

Dear   :

This note offers appreciation for the wonderful job you and our friends at [*name of company*] did in putting on [*event*] for this year's campaign. It was a first-class affair put on by a first-rate organization, and it was an appropriate event to cap off an extraordinary campaign. It simply could not have been better.

In extending to your our appreciation, we would be remiss if we did not also express our gratitude for the long-standing support and fine relationship that has evolved over the past few years between [*name of organization*] and [*company*]. [*Name of organization*] is stronger and better because of your help. For that, we extend our heartfelt appreciation.

Letter 2–12: A thank you letter for volunteer work on a specific project.

Dear   :

As we complete one of our busiest and most successful summers ever, it's time to say thanks to those who helped to make it all possible. As a member of our Chairman's Round Table, you have contributed to our having provided thousands of youth, families, and seniors with experiences that have enriched their lives.

Since you receive our reports regularly, I won't repeat the details of our work here. I have, however, enclosed some thoughts as to how [*name of organization*] is addressing the problems of substance abuse and gang violence. I hope that you'll find it informative.

Of course, we hope that you'll continue your support through the Chairman's Round Table. You have my pledge that your contribution will be used wisely to make our community a better place to live and work.

Letter 2–13: A thank you letter for continuing support.

Dear   :

This note offers our thanks and appreciation for your leadership and work for this year's annual current support campaign.

I know that the spectacular results are probably rewarding enough. However, I wanted to tell you how much we appreciate your willingness to take on the challenge of leading the campaign, which is certainly not an easy job. If it were, we wouldn't need strong leadership in order to accomplish our goals. We are grateful for your help. I am very proud of the results, and I thank you for your willingness to give of your time and talent to assure that we have a strong [*name of organization*] in our community.

Letter 2–14: A thank you letter for campaign leadership.

Dear   :

On behalf of [*name of company*], I would like to extend our deep appreciation for having been chosen to receive the [*name award or certificate*] for this year.

This [*award*] carries with it a great deal of significance because our firm has always wholeheartedly agreed with the aims of the [*Safety Board*]. We are extremely proud.

On behalf of my associates and myself, thank you.

Letter 2–15: A letter of thanks for an award.

Dear   :

I was saddened the other day to find that you will be leaving our area but overjoyed for you and for the opportunity you have taken. We have enjoyed working with you and deeply appreciate all that you have done to support the work of our [*organization's name*]. You have always been a splendid emissary for [*company*], and we have been fortunate to have benefited from our association.

Please accept our heartiest congratulations on your new assignment. You will be missed.

Letter 2–16: A farewell letter to someone who has provided support.

Dear   :

This friendly reminder has been sent to you because in reviewing our list of contributors for this year's support campaign, we noticed that no payment has been made on your pledge of [*dollar amount*].

We wouldn't bother you with this reminder if we didn't understand how easy it is, in this busy world of ours, to let something like this slip by unnoticed.

We also want you to know how important your contribution is to the operation of our organization's programs for [*youth, families, and seniors*] in our community. When pledges are made, we depend on them. That is, we plan programs, hire staff, and purchase supplies and equipment based on the amounts committed.

So you see, your interest in and support of [*organization name*] makes a real difference in the lives of many people and is deeply appreciated. We hope it continues and that you will take this opportunity to drop a check in the mail. (A postage-paid envelope is enclosed for your convenience.)

Letter 2–17: A reminder letter concerning an unpaid donation.

Dear   :

   Please accept our apologies for having sent you a letter regarding [*name of corporation*]'s 19— pledge to our annual support campaign. Our records were simply not updated. It was a grievous error on our part, and we hope that you will accept our sincere apologies that it occurred.

   We also wish to thank you for your continuing support of our organization. We deeply appreciate it and want you to be aware of how much the help of [*person's name*] is recognized and valued by our [*name of organization*]. [*She/he*] is one of a group of volunteers that make possible many of the programs that we operate to benefit [*youth, families, and seniors*] in our community. Thank you for supporting [*her/his*] efforts.

Letter 2–18: An apology letter for a mistake in record-keeping.

Dear   :

Thank you for your recent letter. I'm extremely sorry that you did not find your first experience with us to be more satisfying. Since all who now sign up for programs are enrolled as members, I'm puzzled as to how our policies and practices were interpreted to you. Thanks to your letter, I'm looking into it.

In regard to the camp, the people with whom we scheduled the sessions double-booked and had more groups scheduled than they could handle. In addition, they could not provide us with the required certificate of insurance coverage. We've not experienced these problems in past years. Though the change was beyond our control, we regret any inconvenience or disappointment you and your daughter may have experienced as a result.

In appreciation of your support for our organization, please, at your convenience bring this letter to [*person's name*] in our membership office during regular business hours, and she'll prepare a complimentary community membership card for your daughter. It will be good for one year.

Thank you again for taking the time to write. We will continue to do our very best to remain deserving of your support.

Letter 2–19: An apology letter that offers a gift as reparation.

When an employee angers a customer or a prospect, management should respond immediately (Letter 2–20). One upset customer can undo the goodwill of 1,000 who are satisfied.

Another situation calling for apology is a mistake in the accounting department. Letter 2–21 offers a refreshing approach to the situation. The company admits both the mistake and that it originated not from a computer but from a human error.

The next six letters (2–22 through 2–27) also fall into the apology category; each refers to a different (but common) situation faced by companies.

MOTIVATION LETTERS

While apologies aim to assuage the guilt of the person making the apology (and to inspire forgiveness in the recipient of the apology), guilt can occasionally be used toward positive ends. For example, well-written letters can cause someone to feel guilty about not following through on a job they committed to carrying out. Clearly, the intent in Letter 2–28 is to inspire action on the part of the recipient.

Companies should also regularly send motivational letters to their customers. For example, a personalized note such as Letter 2–29, from the manager of a store, can keep customers coming back.

LETTERS WITH SOMETHING EXTRA

At times, businesspeople run across articles or items in newspapers or magazines that have been written by or about clients, prospects, or friends. The wise businessperson usually clips the article and sends it along with a note such as Letter 2–30.

When selling anything—from seminars to stereos—the opening and verbiage in the letter is critical in determining whether the correspondence gets response or is tossed. Letter 2–31 shows how this might be done in a note inviting a group to a seminar that starts out with an intriguing question.

Following a seminar or sales presentation, thank-you notes enable the writer to mention a benefit to the recipient that may have been forgotten during a sales presentation (Letter 2–32). They also allow the writer to tease the prospect with a remark she or he knows the potential customer is anxious about.

Dear   :

    Please accept my sincere apologies for the unpleasant conversation you had with [*name*].

    [*As we discussed*] our company holds every one of our clients in high esteem, and we value the positive relationship we have built with [*name of company*] during the past [*time period*].

    [*New employee*] has been assigned to handle your account and I think you will find [*her/him*] experienced, conscientious, and extremely courteous.

    If there is any other way in which I can help, please let me know.

    I look forward to seeing you again [*talking to you*] in the near future.

Letter 2–20: A letter apologizing for the behavior of an employee.

Dear   :

We goofed!

I offer my apologies for the mix-up and delay in our accounting department, and I hope that this letter will serve to resolve our recent difficulties.

Apparently, your payment was received, but it was credited to an account that bears a similar name to yours. Therefore, we started sending you our standard notices requesting payment. Even after the posting error was rectified, our accounting department failed to notify our credit department, which is why you continued to receive our correspondence demanding payment.

This error has been corrected, and, once again, please accept my sincere apology for the problems we caused. We value your business and hope to see you again shortly.

In the meantime, if there is any question I can answer, please call.

Letter 2–21: A letter apologizing for an accounting error.

Dear   :

   After some investigation, I believe that we have found the source of the error that led us to our misunderstanding.

   When we received your purchase order, we were unable to fill the order for immediate delivery due to [*why*]. Our letter informing you of this delay and requesting your instructions was mailed the following day. We did not receive a reply, so we proceeded to send a follow-up letter to you on [*date*].

   We have been able to deliver the order since [*date*], but felt that because you had emphasized "for immediate delivery" on your purchase order, we should wait for your authorization before shipping.

   We are extremely sorry for the delay and any inconvenience it might have caused.

Letter 2–22: A letter apologizing for a purchase order error.

Dear   :

There is no doubt that apologies from us are in order.

When we assumed management of the [*name of business*], we were provided with a list of accounts payable and accounts receivable. While we attempted to obtain verification of these accounts, we obviously failed to contact you.

While the previous manager erred by showing your account as a receivable, we compounded the error by failing to verify the account before we handed it over to the collection agency.

While I wish I were able to lay all of the blame on my predecessor, I must acknowledge my responsibility and apologize to you for the inconvenience and embarrassment. I have contacted the collection agency and explained completely. You will not be hearing from them again regarding this matter.

If there is anything else I can do, please let me know.

Once again, my heartfelt apologies.

Letter 2–23: A letter apologizing for a mistake that occurred when the company changed over to new management.

Dear   :

It does happen—even to [*profession*] who are supposed to remember everything! When my secretary told me that your office had called to inform me that I had missed my appointment, I couldn't believe it. I rechecked my calendar, which indicated the appointment was for tomorrow, [*date*]. I don't know how this mix-up occurred, but please accept my apology for the inconvenience it must have caused.

I would appreciate it if we could reschedule our meeting for next week, if possible.

I'll call to see if we can set a mutually convenient time.

Letter 2–24: A letter apologizing for a missed appointment.

Dear   :

    Our computer erred—or at least the humans who input information did so. There is no doubt that you were charged twice for the above-referenced invoice. We rectified the situation by crediting your account, as you can see by the enclosed statement.

    Please accept my apologies for any inconvenience. I can assure you we are doing everything possible to make sure it doesn't happen again.

Letter 2–25: A letter apologizing for a double charge.

Dear   :

   We sincerely apologize for the mix-up that caused you to cancel your order. This letter also acknowledges receipt of your letter of [*date*], in which you stated your reasons for canceling.

   I am extremely sorry about the misunderstanding and have taken the matter up with management to ensure that it does not occur again.

   As one of our valued customers, your satisfaction is our primary concern. Please accept our apology.

Letter 2–26: A letter apologizing for a mistake that caused an order cancellation.

Dear   :

Thank you for clarifying the problem we have been experiencing with your account. The information you provided has enabled us to trace the error, which was definitely our fault.

We are presently under new management and are confident that the changes will eliminate the need to write a letter such as this in the future.

Please accept our apology for the inconvenience this mix-up has caused.

We thank you for your patience and assistance and look forward to serving you in the near future.

Letter 2–27: A letter acknowledging and apologizing for a management error.

Dear   :

   We've missed you at our campaign report breakfasts. I hope that you'll be in attendance at our Victory Breakfast this Wednesday, February 22, 7:00 A.M. at [*place*]. We have a lot to celebrate!

   Of course, if you can finalize your accounts and report the results at the Victory Breakfast, it will add immensely to our success and lift our spirits even higher.

Letter 2–28: A letter encouraging more active participation.

Dear   :

Wouldn't it be nice to be able to buy all of your gifts this holiday season without having to worry about paying for them—until next March?

We thought it would, and we decided this would be a perfect way to say thank you to our premier customers for having shopped with us throughout the year.

Starting today, any purchases that you charge to your account will not appear on your statement until next March! You can take advantage of the offer until Christmas Eve [*year*].

We hope that you will take advantage of our holiday offering and come see our seasonal selections. Also, while you are here, please come up to the fourth floor for a complimentary glass of eggnog.

I look forward to seeing you.

Letter 2–29: A letter from a retail company tempting consumers with unique offers.

Dear   :

My congratulations on the fascinating article you wrote in the [*date*] issue of [*name of publication*].

The study you presented was quite informative and highly entertaining, a combination that is rarely found in articles of this nature. You are to be commended for your writing ability as well as the recognized inroads you have made in your field of expertise.

Thank you for sharing your findings with us in such a delightful manner.

Letter 2–30: This letter of congratulation would be sent with a clipped article written by the client.

Dear   :

Does the high cost of doing business bother you?

Many large firms have turned to the telephone as a means to save money and generate additional profits. As a businessperson with a large work force, you will be interested in our seminar covering the pros and cons (as well as the laws and procedures) of telephone soliciting.

The seminar will provide you with facts to assist you in making a decision. Many of those invited are current customers who have requested this seminar. Others were selected based on the size and nature of their business. Incidentally, I guarantee you that there will be no solicitation of your business at our seminar.

We welcome you and your questions. I have enclosed the time, location, and agenda of the program for your review.

Letter 2–31: A letter announcing a seminar. Note the key opening line and the guarantee that the client will not be solicited at the seminar.

Dear   :

　　Thank you for the opportunity you gave me to discuss your group insurance program and needs on the telephone today.

　　As to the question you asked about service, let me assure you that we provide excellent follow-up to policy holders. Our present clients would be happy to testify to that fact.

　　Frankly, until we have an opportunity to meet with you and confirm what type of coverage you presently have and might want for the future, it is impossible for me to say whether our rates would be lower than those you are currently paying. We do, however, have several programs available which we know are extremely competitive with other group carriers.

　　I'll call to see if we can set up a mutually convenient time.

Letter 2–32: A thank you note that invites further discussion of programs previously introduced.

Don't wait for a presentation to send a thank-you note, however. A simple thank-you note is good business practice regardless of the industry or the event. It not only makes the recipient feel good, but it also keeps the relationship open.

CHAPTER **3**

The Four-Step Sales Formula

Two years from now, your business could be worth
two and a half to twenty-five times what it is worth
today . . . or you could fall into the list of business
also-rans . . . the choice is yours.

Provocative? Of course, but aside from stirring emotions, it does what the lead on every letter should do: It gets the reader's attention. The first rule in letter writing is that the lead has to grab the reader's attention. Whether it is an internal memo concerning a promotion or a letter to a supplier, customer, prospect, or acquaintance, the trademark of a good letter is that the lead sentence or paragraph stands out.

THE UNIVERSAL FEATURE OF LETTERS: SALES

In reality, every letter is a sales letter. Although the product may not be an automobile, insurance policy, or marketing program, every letter is selling something. It could be image, involvement in a local charity, or support for a cause.

Effective sales letters are no different than well-put-together advertisements. They follow a specific structure that is designed to attract attention and generate action on the part of the recipient. In advertising, four words comprise a winning structure:

1. Attention
2. Interest
3. Desire
4. Action

Before anything happens, the writer has to grab the reader's attention. In print advertising, this is usually done through provocative headlines, such as

Grow or Die . . .
$495 Transcript for only $39 . . .
I've got to get this off my chest before I explode . . .

How much money does Joe's business make . . .

What's the easiest way to make money . . .

How can you boost productivity without adding cost . . .

Did you ever ask yourself why you bought it? . . .

Seeing Is Believing . . .

The Lazy Man's Way to Riches

Each of these headlines was on an extremely successful advertisement and although each sold a different product or service, they all share on thing: the headline or lead is provocative and captures the reader's interest.

Good letters and memos use the same process. Opening lines must grab *attention*, the next sentence or two should spark the reader's *interest*, the next paragraph or two should create a *desire* (on the part of the reader), and the last part should cause the reader to take some *action*.

MASTERING THE OPENING: ADDRESSING NEEDS

Openings are usually the toughest part of the letter for writers to master. Many letter writers spend half their time working on the lead and the rest on the remainder of the letter. The same is true of memos. Get off on the right foot, and the rest of the correspondence flows. Take, for instance, these lead sentences. They were used for specific products and companies, but they could be transferred to almost any product and service.

- My boss would kill me if he found out I was writing you this letter, but I want to prove a point to him.

- If your practice isn't where you'd like it to be, perhaps you're not marketing it the way you could or should.

- The congressional tax bill will affect more than just individual and corporate tax returns. It will affect you because the investment rules you have been playing by are going to change . . . radically.

- There are seven practical ways you can add an extra $ _____ to $ _____ to your income.

- What I'm about to explain to you is not understood by 1 in 1,000 service company owners.

- It was a wonderful visit for me, and I thank you for your exceptional hospitality.
- Confused about which new _____ to buy?
- Forget everything you've heard about the _____ .
- This letter may determine the future of your business.
- In the next 20 seconds, you will read something that may mean an enormous difference to your business in the coming year.

Sales letters qualify as being good when they talk about the customer's (or recipient's) needs rather than the writer's. The writer must try to put her- or himself in the place of the recipient. Ask yourself questions such as the following:

- What does the prospect need?
- What are his or her primary concerns?
- What doubts might he or she have?
- What financial considerations does he or she have?
- Have there been problems in the past that may concern him or her?
- What is (are) his or her goals?

THE AIDA FORMAT

The following letters illustrate the ingredients it takes to write a successful sales letter. Each follows the AIDA (attention, interest, desire, action) format. In some cases, the entire letter is reprinted, but in others, only portions of the correspondence appear. Each area is labeled either Attention, Interest, Desire, or Action.

Attention

Dear   :

I wrote you a couple of weeks ago but want to send this letter again because it is so important.

This is the opening line of a letter from former President Jimmy Carter to potential donors for a charity. Obviously, a letter with an impressive letterhead and bearing the president's name is going to attract attention. Now that he has the reader's attention, he goes on to try to spark interest.

Interest

> As a former U.S. President, I have been asked to lend my name to the work of many fine and worthy causes.
>
> When Rosalynn and I talked about this, we decided that we wanted to be part of something that would make a lasting difference in people's lives. Something that would mean more than just the use of our name on an organization's letterhead.

The reader knows from the tone of the letter that the former President is involved in something, but what? By not revealing the cause until later in the correspondence, the writer is able to keep the reader's interest . . . and keep him or her reading.

> After much thought, we chose to support the work of Habitat for Humanity. And since then, I have served on Habitat's board of directors. In our book, *Everything to Gain*, we write in detail about our experiences with Habitat for Humanity, as an example of how to add excitement and challenge to one's life.
>
> Let me tell you why I feel so strongly about the good work Habitat is doing.
>
> As President, I had firsthand knowledge of just how serious and dehumanizing the housing problems of the poor and disadvantaged really were. I was shocked and appalled!

Is President Carter keeping the reader's interest? By this time, the reader knows it is going to be some kind of pitch for a charity. This is a point where the reader can be lost, but the writer uses a clever device—storytelling. Everyone is fascinated by a good story. We've been telling stories for thousands of years, and there is no better place to put one (as long as it is brief) than a letter. It keeps the reader interested.

> Today, hundreds of thousands of families right here in America live in the most deplorable housing conditions imaginable: roach- and rat-infested ghetto flats; dilapidated rural shacks; decaying, crumbling old apartments.
>
> One of those families was the Strongs—Ruby, Oscar and

their five children—all struggling to get by in a cramped little shack in Sumner, Mississippi.

The letter goes on to chronicle the accomplishments of Habitat, which increases the interest and desire of the reader to help. The actual pitch for funds does not come until the letter is almost at the end.

Desire

Right now we need 1 million people who are each willing to give at least $20 to share in the life-changing accomplishments of this exciting and desperately needed work.

Through the visionary work of Habitat for Humanity, the dream of adequate low-cost housing for the disadvantaged is becoming a reality. It's happening in the spirit of Christian love, and it's not costing one red cent of taxpayer's money. To me, that's one great investment!

Action

I urge you to join Rosalynn and me in this vitally important work. Whatever you can send—$20, $50, or more will make a big difference.

Gratefully yours

Jimmy Carter

P.S. I know of no better investment to help restore human dignity than to help someone else like the Strong family. Please join me with your gift. Thank you.

At some point in every letter, the writer has to ask for the money, the sale, the involvement, or whatever. When this section is written, writers should remember to give readers limited choices. The fewer the choices, the better the chance of success. For example, ask for a specific dollar amount, not just a donation.

Attention

Dear New Mother:

As a mother, there are precious moments none of us will ever forget. The first cry you heard; the first time you held your baby; the day you both came home.

This opening line from a direct-mail company to new mothers captivated attention in order to sell unusual baby-picture frames. Few sales letters are in a more competitive field than direct mail.

Interest

The pleasure of those memories is difficult to describe, especially when it comes to relating them to someone who has never felt the joy of being a mother.

The mother's interest is heightened as she remembers the actual experience she had.

Desire

Now, you can capture and relive those moments forever with our special "birth celebration baby frame." This beautiful keepsake holds your favorite baby picture forever. And engraved on the birthframe is your baby's birthdate, weight, time of birth and, yes, even length.

Here's the chance for the mother to own one herself or to give one as a gift. The desire is heightened.

It is a marvelous, nostalgic gift for grandparents, relatives, and close friends. It also serves as a delightful reminder of that wonderful day and moment when your baby arrived.

The "birth celebration baby frame": a carefully crafted work of art that will allow you to remember those magical moments forever.

Sincerely,

Marianne Majors

Action

P.S. For a limited time, we will do the engraving on the frame at no cost. Take advantage of this special bonus and call toll free to [number] or send [amount] to [address]. The "birth celebration frame" comes with a money-back guarantee.

The request for action (a sales order) on the part of the customer is saved until last. However, once the writer does ask for a commitment, there is no wishy-washiness about it. The prospect is *told* to take advantage of it, not *asked.* The money-back guarantee plays an important role in assuring the buyer that the product is good and her money is safe.

Attention

Dear   :

You're going to love this letter.

It's your chance for fame, fortune, and whatever else your heart has ever desired. (Well, so I'm exaggerating.)

In the opening line of this letter from one service company to another the writer dangles something of value in front of the readers and captivates their attention by doing so. The writer also challenges the readers by telling them that they are going to love the letter. The challenge is enough of an attraction to cause the readers to continue.

Interest

Actually, this letter is an opportunity . . . and it will not cost you a dime. . . . At the same time, it may help generate clients . . . if you want any.

Here's the pitch . . . I'm doing . . .

The writer describes the project and tells readers what kind of help is wanted. Still keeping the readers' interest, the writer explains what will be given to readers who respond:

Desire

In return, I would pay tribute to you in a special acknowledgment section and would also quote you throughout the book. The book is being targeted to executives and major companies, which could, of course, lead to inquiries.

Wouldn't the recipients like a special tribute?

Action

Sound interesting? I'll call your office the week of [*date*] to see what you think.

Attention

Dear   :

As the president of the _____ Chamber of Commerce, please accept my sincere appreciation for your membership support since [*year*].

This letter was sent with an overdue bill for the recipient's membership, but the overdue bill is not, of course, mentioned in the opening. That would be a sure way to lose the reader. Before collecting money, the writer has to get the reader's attention. It helps that the businessperson is getting a letter from the president of the chamber, not the accounting department. The note from the president heightens interest, whereas a letter from the accounting department would probably end up in the trash before the reader even finished the first paragraph.

Interest

As a member of the Board, I have had a first-hand opportunity to see how the Chamber has impacted the economy of our city, as well as the well-being of members such as yourself.

Now the writer is talking about something that interests the reader directly. Remember, in all letters, the recipient's needs should be addressed. How does—and can—the Chamber benefit the member? Can the reader profit from the relationship? With those thoughts in mind, the writer continues:

The Chamber operates on two fronts—it advocates the views of its member firms and opposes taxation and anti-business legislation.

In the coming year, our efforts will be concentrated on transportation, housing, retail sales, jobs, worker's compensation, increasing sales for local service businesses, and air quality control.

The member's business is bound to fit into one or more of the categories. His interest is still with the letter.

Desire

Your firm has been an important part of the growing economy of our city. It has been involved on a daily basis and has contributed greatly to the city's well-being.

The reader has been flattered and has come to the realization that her or his company is important to the community and chamber. The reader wants to continue that involvement. With that in mind, the writer hits home with the action that must be taken by the businessperson.

Action

Therefore, I would greatly appreciate your approval of the enclosed membership renewal.

Cordially,

Attention

Dear Publisher:

If you've got a healthy supply of your latest directories gathering dust in some warehouse, here's a sensible way to convert all those books into cash in the next six weeks.

In this opening line, the writer is trying to sell the publisher a marketing program. Most firms with inventory would be anxious to convert it to cash. The letter focuses on a basic business need: cash.

Interest

I'll create a powerful space ad and/or sales letter offering this year's directory at an attractive discount over the regular published price—the precise discount we end up offering is up to you. By adopting this "sale" approach in space ads and/or developing a potent direct mail letter that we send to a list of the best possible prospects as well as all of your past directory buyers, I believe we can quickly move about 1,000 directories (possibly many more) in a matter of weeks.

In this letter, the *attention* portion is short, but the *interest* goes on for three to four paragraphs. The *desire* portion runs three or four paragraphs as well.

Desire

I won't take a penny in up-front payment. Instead I want 25% of the sales revenue emanating from my ads and letters. I ask only two things: (1) That you put up a minimum amount of test money. (2) That we use an independent bank trust account to handle the responses.

Accept these two reasonable requests and I will create a breakthrough advertising approach capable of liquidating all your current book inventory in a relatively short period of time.

This intriguing offer would interest most publishers. Now for the close, or the *action* section.

Action

If you are interested in accepting my lucrative proposition, call or write me at the address below. Concurrently, send me a copy of your latest directory, including samples of all recent sales literature, ads, and direct mail you've successfully used in the past. Our dealings will be treated with strictest confidence.

If we get started in the next two weeks, I can probably produce a lot of money for you before the middle of November.

Sincerely,

P.S. If you don't want to sell directories at discount, we can also develop new subscriber ads and solicitations, as well as create pieces to reactivate old buyers. I can also increase most publishers' renewal rate by as much as 40%.

P.P.S. There are also numerous synergistic products and services we could cross-sell to your current and expired subscriber base without jeopardizing the viability of those names. We can explore these more exotic profit opportunities when we talk.

The P.S. and P.P.S. are designed to create additional desire. The reason that they are placed at the end of the letter is discussed later in this chapter, along with the purpose of postscripts and how they should be used.

Action

Dear Dr.   :

If your practice isn't where you'd like it to be, perhaps you're not marketing it the way you could or should.

The opening line in this letter to professionals (in which the writer has a marketing program to sell), captivates the reader by appealing to the recipient's needs.

Interest

For example, if you're not getting as many new clients or patients as you'd like to or ought to, there are a few very effective things you could do immediately.

The writer follows with a number of practical marketing ideas that the professional could use. Many of these could be implemented by the professional without help, but others would require help in order to be carried out. The ideas help to pique the reader's interest:

You could speak at local industry, trade, business, civic, or church gatherings on your area of expertise.

You could instantly arrange to be interviewed on a local radio show.

You could make arrangements with your local newspaper to write regular articles which are fully credited to you.

An interesting approach in a sales letter is to outline something that a prospect could (or should) be doing. The prospect sees the suggestion and understands its value but is unable to carry it out alone. The prospect needs help. In other words, the ideas within the letter are not simple enough for the professional to just pick up and use without help—the help the prospect would receive from the marketing professional writing the letter.

Desire

There are enormous marketing possibilities and opportunities available to you in your practice without ever compromising your integrity or sacrificing your professionalism.

I've just completed a new, two-volume report telling you

how to take advantage of over 500 different marketing, promotional, PR, and advertising opportunities for your practice—irrespective of what level of success or maturity your practice is at right now.

For example:

The writer spells out a half-dozen marketing possibilities and then goes on to outline 21 additional techniques that the professional could use to increase business. The writer next points out a few other things to increase the professional's desire.

Your practice is a profit-oriented business.

You have rent to pay. Payroll to meet. Clients to service. New business to develop. Attrition and bad debt to contend with. Taxes. Fees. Overhead galore. And you, as much as any commercial or industrial type businessman or woman, have to contend with this.

I believe this two-part report on "How to Profitably Market Your Professional Services" can realistically be worth a 20% increase in your personal income in the next 18 months alone. And if you are the slightest bit ambitious, you could amass far greater achievements.

Action

Now comes the price. It's $195 for both volumes. This is either a lot of money or a pittance depending on what you compare it with.

If this were just another mono-dimensional report on some mundane aspect of your practice, it'd probably be worth a lot less.

But if someone can teach you to bring in twice as many clients or patients, how much is that worth? If someone can show you how to double the profits from clients or patients you currently service, what's that worth to you?

The recipient is told about a 90-day money-back guarantee, as well as the ability to use a charge card for the program. (Charge cards improve response anywhere from 10 to 20 percent.)

Attention

Dear   :

I hope your vacation was a good one . . . welcome back!

The organization that wrote this opening line wants to get the recipient of the correspondence involved in a charitable activity. When asking someone to participate in something, it is a good idea to try to add something in the note of a nonbusiness nature, such as the vacation. It establishes rapport between the writer and the recipient.

Interest

Now that you're back, I wanted to remind you we need your help.

Desire

We have to set up a finish-the-job campaign and need you for it.

Action

We need you to contact the folks at _____. I won't be in the office until next week, however, I would be more than happy to discuss it with you so we could plan strategy.

Attention

Dear   :

Did Ponce de León really discover a fountain of youth in Florida or did he merely have a great public relations man?

This letter is from a firm trying to sell its services to another company. The opening line is intriguing and hard for anyone to ignore.

Interest

We will probably never know the answer. So many questions like this one still remain because they have come about through word-of-mouth and not historical fact. Word-of-mouth has, more than anything else, the power to create legends.

Desire

Contemporary—as well as historical—legends are created all the time. In fact, our firm has been responsible for many of our present-day legends. By placing articles in local and national publications, and on radio and television, we have turned many obscure people and companies into celebrities and well-known firms. We can do the same for you.

Action

I'd like the opportunity of speaking with you for a few moments and outlining the type of programs we have created for others in your field. I will call next week to see if we might set up a mutually convenient time. Thank you for your time and interest.

A short, extremely well-done letter designed to open the door of a prospective client. It also shows that letters need not be lengthy in order to spark interest on the part of a potential client. This writer has mastered the AIDA approach in four paragraphs. This same letter can be adapted for other service companies and used with prospective clients.

Attention

Dear   :

While it would be easy to place the blame on our computer, the poor fellow has received enough abuse since joining our firm, so someone else must assume the responsibility for the mistake made with your order—me.

This letter apologizes to customers for delays in getting refunds to them. The opening line is refreshing in that the writer is not trying to blame the problem on a computer. This letter may not be selling a specific product, but it is selling the company's image, which is certainly an important transaction.

Interest

Frankly, I goofed. Please accept my apology for the error and (if our computer behaves) I will try to avoid making the same mistake again.

Desire

Our bookkeeping department has been told to issue a refund check to you, and you could receive it within the next few days.

Action

Once again, I apologize for any inconvenience. If you do not receive your check by the end of next week, please let me know and I will look into it to make sure our computer isn't passing around a virus.

In answering complaints, many firms try to blame the problem on something that is beyond their control. Consumers are more sophisticated than ever, and they read through smoke screens. In most cases, it is best simply to tell the truth.

The truth often prompts the buyer–customer to forgive and forget. It is when a company refuses to take responsibility for its actions that it can turn troubles with customers into a crisis.

Attention

Dear   :

How would you like a complete collection of 14 special situation reports worth $125 absolutely free?

The free offer in the opening line of this subscription pitch from a newsletter publisher is something few can resist. *Free* is one of the most potent words in advertising.

Interest

The situation reports cover everything from the investment lessons of 1980 to a 95-page research report on the outlook for the economy, plus seven investment exposés.

Desire

All these reports are yours to keep and enjoy—and hopefully profit from.

Action

Everything is yours free, when you accept our irresistible

offer to let us send you two rare and desirable U.S. silver dollars worth over $20 wholesale for just $19 total!

The letter goes on for another page describing the benefits of the reports and the value of the coins. It closes with a lengthy P.S. and P.P.S.

P.S. In case you're wondering what the two-coin silver dollar set we'll be sending you for $19 is comprised of, you get a Peace silver dollar of the 1922 or 1923 vintage and we'll also include a choice Morgan silver dollar from the 1921 period. These are circulated silver dollars in very good condition, or better, with 3/4 of an ounce of silver each—1 1/2 ounces of silver content alone—in your $19 set.

P.P.S. If you've always wanted to own a few rare coins but have been afraid to call a coin dealer for fear they'd strong-arm you into buying rolls and rolls or even a bag of coins you did not want, this is a wonderfully nonthreatening way for you to get two of the most popular prized U.S. rare coins of all for really no risk whatsoever. You can hold them, touch them and reflect on their history, rarity and unique form of art and beauty without any pressure to ever buy again. I think this is one opportunity you should definitely take advantage of.

Typical letters seldom have a P.S. this lengthy. However, when companies try to generate business through the mail, it takes a significant amount of copy to convince the prospect to put his or her money in an envelope. Thus, mail-order letters are usually longer than non-mail-order correspondence.

Attention

Dear   :

You can have this $595 service free for one year.

Everyone knows that nothing is free, but the offer in this opening line from an investment company to prospects is intriguing and captures the attention of the recipient.

Interest

It's the most expensive telephone number in the world.
That's right, in the Cayman Islands you would pay $595 for

this number. The number, however, entitles you to talk to Mr. X. Who is Mr. X? He's a citizen of the world who unequivocably predicts runaway inflation and a major U.S. banking collapse.

Desire

When? Where? Well, in the Caymans if you paid $595 you would find out, however, we are offering the same service to you at no cost.

You do not have to go to the Caymans to get this kind of high level inside information. Now there is a new and unique newsletter that comes directly from the Grand Cayman Island. It is called "The Grand Cayman Flash Report" and is unlike any newsletter anywhere.

The editors of the newsletter are brutal. They believe the banking system is going down the tubes so fast it will make a ride on the Titanic seem like a pleasure cruise.

Here are some of the articles you will find in this completely different newsletter:

- Little-known ways to keep your assets and investments out of the control of the government.
- How some investors turn $2,000 into $30,000 by investing in a commodity that most don't even think about.
- The upcoming elections, their impact and how to prepare for them.

Action

"The Grand Cayman Flash Report" costs $138 for a one-year subscription. If you subscribe now, I will enroll you at one-half that price. In other words, you will receive this unique newsletter for one full year for only $69.

The letter goes on with additional bonus products that are given to whose who subscribe. In all, the letter ran seven pages. (Remember that to get someone to commit to something by mail takes more convincing than a face-to-face confrontation.) The benefits took up more than half the copy. It closes with a dual P.S.

P.S. Those free reports are amazing. Please take a moment to read about them on the yellow fact sheet. Thank you.

P.P.S. Subscribers who took Mr. X's hotline advice in January would have made $3,000 on a single silver contract and $1,300 in gold in just two weeks.

Following is the opening line of a letter from financial analyst to a prospective client.

Attention

Dear   :

I have attached a dollar to the top of this letter for two reasons:

Few things grab more attention than a coin or dollar bill at the top of a letter. It shows that the writer is interested and committed to the reader.

Interest

I have something very important to tell you and I needed some way to catch your attention.

Because what I am writing about concerns money, I thought a little financial eye-catcher was especially appropriate.

Desire

My name is _____ and on March 13, my staff hand-selected and taught 189 people from all over the country my secrets to wealth. Within 60 days, those people had profited an average of $12,916 per person.

The same staff will be in _____ on January 5–14 and they would like to meet with you on a personal basis.

On those days they will reveal, to a select group of people, a new way to make money in real estate.

With the changing economic climate, now is the best time to buy real estate. If you are interested in high-cash-flow real estate, spending the day with these specialists could be worth a virtual fortune to you. In fact, we personally guarantee your success. Not only will you learn the latest techniques of real estate investing from us but you must make $10,000 or more in the period of one year or we will refund your tuition!

Action

> I have enclosed a ticket to reserve your seat and free reports. All you have to do is call and confirm your reservation. Pre-register with your MasterCard or Visa when you call, and the cost of tuition is only $39. Call and pre-register before January 4 and you will receive this additional bonus:

The letter closes with an interesting P.S. The writer implies (and hopes that the reader gets the message) that the reports are valuable, attendance is high, and space is tight. There may even be a waiting list. It adds to the urgency of the letter.

> P.S. Please let us know even if you cannot come so the reports reserved for you can be released to someone else.
>
> Thank you.

Attention

Following is the opening line from a service company to some of its clients.

> Dear   :
>
> I was searching for a special way to express my good wishes to you for the holidays . . . and I found one.

Interest

> I discovered that there are some things in life that cannot be improved on. One is for someone to sincerely wish someone else their best wishes for a happy, healthy and prosperous holiday season and a joyful new year.
>
> In conjunction with that wish, which I send to you and your family, our company is making a donation in your family's name to _____. I think those less fortunate than we will be extremely grateful to you for thinking of them at this holiday season.

Desire

> To those at your company, and to your friends and relatives all of us at _____ say, "Happy Holidays." Enjoy yourselves. May the years ahead be bright and joyful.

Action

As part of our traditional celebration, we are hosting a get-together at our facilities on [*date*]. We would like to extend a warm holiday welcome to you, your management and your family. Please join us.

This holiday greeting is unusual, but it nevertheless has impact. It gives something unexpected to a valued customer and invites the customer to a gathering, which is an excellent approach for any firm to use. The note stands out for another reason: It does not go on and on. Holiday messages should be short. They should not be two page letters.

Attention

Dear   :

Hello, Dali!

Or how a $500,000 snafu resulted in your getting the chance to own the perfect "twin" of a famous $27,500 lithograph for a mere $195.

That intriguing opening line would stop most readers. It goes on to talk about the artist Salvadore Dali.

Interest

Almost everyone interested in fine art and modern day masters knows and admires the work of the late Salvador Dali, the man most artists consider to be the pioneer of European surrealism.

Dali lived in art history as the man who made the most inventive and enduring contributions to the principles of surrealism.

The description of Dali and his contributions to art go on for more than a page. The writer then begins to turn to Dali's actual paintings.

Dali's oil paintings sold for as much as $5 million before his death. And his watercolors went for $500,000 plus.

His signed lithographs fetched an easy $25,000 plus and that was for some of the lesser-known pieces.

After his death everything skyrocketed. American Express acquired a complete run of 5,000 of Dali's watercolor prints and sold them out in record time for $925 each—unframed.

The letter goes on for another page, citing instance after instance of Dali paintings that soared in price. The object is to convince the prospect that the paintings appreciate significantly and to slowly build a desire on the part of the recipient for one of the paintings.

Desire

Now comes the best part of my story. I have a good friend . . .

The writer goes on to explain that he has obtained a number of Dali prints that can be sold at an extraordinarily low price. Each sells for $220, but the most intriguing part of the letter is an offer the writer makes to those who purchase the prints. He is guaranteeing the art. If you don't like it, return it. It is another way to say "money-back guarantee."

Action

Then, once you've determined that what I am offering is a wonderful bargain on a beautiful and prized piece of famous art, return the completed order form immediately.

Finally, to make the purchase risk-free, I have decided to allow you up to 60 days to hang your Dali in your home or office and make absolutely certain you love it.

To order your lithograph, on a first-come, first-served basis, complete the coupon below or call toll free [telephone number].

Another sales letter took a similar tack.

Attention

Dear   :

What single investment appreciated approximately 450% greater than bonds, 398% higher than stocks, 175% better than homes, and 74% more than diamonds?

That interesting question is bound to attract the reader's attention.

Interest

The answer—the Luger World War II Military S/42 hand-gun—one of the growing number of collection-worthy firearms gaining investor attention.

The answer is surprising and hard to believe. It sparks the reader's interest but also causes the reader to question the attention-getting lead. To alleviate those concerns, the writer has to go on and prove to the reader that the gun did appreciate that rapidly.

Let's be more precise. Let's take a careful look at the Luger WWII Military S/42, a desirable investment gun, though far from the most coveted.

We all know that oil compounded at a rate of nearly 18% per year. The Luger S/42 outpaced oil by 80% in the same five year period.

The letter compares the Luger against other investments and shows how well the gun has done. It also talks about the gun's liquidity.

Desire

Would you like to know more about collecting guns? If the answer is yes, we'd like to send you two valuable collections of material. The first is a profit-provoking . . .

Action

Simply return the enclosed card. Or call us toll free at [*telephone number*].

The letter closes with a P.S.

P.S. Remember, guns have been proven winners for years. Find out if they have a place in your investment portfolio.

This still may be hard for consumers to believe, so the writer offers a free catalog in a postpostscript.

Attention

The following clever, entertaining opening is actually from a jewelry company to its customers.

Dear   :

Nope! You guessed wrong, I'm not down under in Australia visiting Crocodile Dundee—though I bet it would be fun!

Interest

I'm actually in a pristine clean laboratory in Japan watching some brilliant scientists duplicate mother nature. Around me are several rows of very high tech, space-age vacuum cleaners. If I didn't know better, I would say it was a set for a science fiction movie.

Inside these vacuum cleaners an almost unbelievable phenomenon is taking place—opals are growing!

I look through the windows to each chamber, but it doesn't appear that anything is happening. There is a good reason. The opals grow so laboriously slowly that it takes almost six months for a full crystal to form.

Desire

But, [*name of prospect*], the wait is worth it. Our opals are 10% more brilliant than one of the best mineral opals for which you would have to pay in excess of $3,000. Our simulated opal of the same size will retail for $100.

And they are more durable too. Unlike mined opals, our opals are not affected by water or heat. They will last many lifetimes. Look at the enclosed brochure and you'll see how beautiful they are.

Sincerely,

Action

P.S. Our opal will not be available to the public until November, however, since you are a regular client, you can buy as many as you want right now at 40% off the regular price. We must receive your order before November 1. This is our way of saying thank you for being such a good customer.

The *action*, or close, has everything in it: *Special* customers get *special* treatment. Order *now*.

Attention

Dear   :

My boss would kill me if he found out I was writing you this letter, but I want to prove a point to him.

Without question, the lead attracts the reader's attention and causes the reader to continue.

Interest

I work for a man many believe is a marketing genius. I can't say for sure—but I do know that his marketing accomplishments are usually amazing. I've worked for him a short 15 months yet in that time I've actually witnessed him save ten struggling companies from near certain failure—with simple, little tricks that were so logical I hit myself for not thinking of them.

But you know, that's his greatest talent. The man's so extraordinarily logical. And frankly, few entrepreneurs approach their marketing problems in a logical common-sense pragmatic manner.

The *interest* builds for nearly a page, citing the myriad accomplishments of the letter-writer's boss.

Desire

Jay does not think magazines would be interested in his marketing perspective.

[*Name of prospect*], how could you not be interested in the commentary of a man who singularly accounted for $965 million in sales in 19__ alone?

I personally think his PR agency is letting him down. That is why I am writing you this letter.

Action

I ask you to read both of the articles I have included. I assure you, you'll be fascinated by their content. Then after reading them, if you wish to reprint either, please do. Or if you want Jay to write a special article for you write me and I promise he'll do it.

The letter closes with several postscripts which contributed to a campaign that generated surprising results. The writer showed clips from three major newspapers that did stories on her boss. None, incidentally, used the material that was sent verbatim, but the interviews did come through.

> P.S. If you are interested, Jay can write articles on additional subjects such as direct marketing, direct mail, mail order, magazine, newsletter and book publishing, intangibles marketing, consumer and business book marketing, seminar promotion, investor lead generating, telephone marketing, advertising and acquisitions.
>
> P.P.S. If you do use one of Jay's articles could you send us a tear sheet . . . we're always interested in finding out who is interested in us. Thank you.

Overdue accounts are problems in almost every business. This firm takes a slightly different approach with this reminder letter.

Attention

> Dear   :
>
> Would you believe that I hate writing letters such as this one? And I know you certainly can't enjoy hearing from me under these circumstances.

Interest

> I am, of course, referring to the fact that your account has fallen significantly behind. Paying bills is something all of us hate to take time to do. However, as a valued customer I would personally urge you to check your payables and see how far in arrears your company happens to be.

Desire

> What makes it extremely difficult is that our new line is about to be released. We view it as one of the best lines we have ever come up with and anticipate record-breaking sales.
>
> I am anxious for your firm to participate in the new line; however, I am unable to continue to extend credit unless we are able to settle some of the invoices that are long past due.

Action

I need a favor from you . . . could you call me this week
[*date*]. Let's discuss your account and see how we might
remedy it so your firm can participate in what is going to be
an exciting and profitable new season.

I look forward to hearing from you.

This low-key collection letter dangles a carrot (the new line) in
front of the debtor. If the letter fails to generate results, a second
version is sent. It is more formal and has a harsher tone.

Attention

Dear   :

Because of the seriousness of your delinquency, and the failure of your firm to respond to our requests, we will be including the name of your company in our national debtor file.

Interest

The file is sent to our list of national vendors and suppliers.
They, in turn, report the findings to any vendors and businesses with which they have transactions.

Desire

I would certainly like to avoid sending the information to
the file. However, at this time, there is only one way for that
to happen—full payment of the overdue account.

Action

If this is feasible, please call me immediately. The national
debtor file will be updated and sent out on [*date*], so I must
hear from you before then.

The lead line in a solicitation letter from a newsletter publisher
certainly has an unusual angle:

Attention

Dear   :

I have a tax problem and I want you to be the beneficiary
instead of the IRS.

Interest

My business had a great year so far in 19__. In fact, we've done so well I'm probably going to pay three times more corporate tax than I did last year. And if we make more money this year the tax problem will only be worse—and I'll have to pay even more money to the IRS.

Desire

I have decided to offer you newsletters and special reports and only charge you the basic cost. Just enough to pay the publisher and the costs needed to process your order. Not a dime more.

For a $77–250 newsletter, this comes to $13–25. I know that's hard to believe, but it is what I am going to do. Here are a few examples to illustrate what I mean . . .

This is the first time I have ever done this. It is really good business sense on my part, too. My customers order an average of three times a year. The average order is $50. If I make a great bargain available to them, I think each will appreciate the discounts and bargains and will end up buying more publications.

In fact, I think they will buy in droves next year if I give them the bargain of the century now.

The way I see it, it only costs the IRS money, not me. I also make customers happy.

Action

On the enclosed flyer you will find a complete list of all the newsletters I can offer . . . and the lowest price I can offer to you . . .

I hope my investment in you, my valued customers, pays off. It seems a lot better investment than giving it to the government.

Warmly,

P.S. One final thing. To make my offer absolutely irresistible, I'm giving you this special bonus: Order three or more newsletters and you may choose any one of the special reports free of charge. The reports supply you with the most exciting wealth-building techniques. They normally cost as much as $30 each but you may choose any one as your free gift.

The *action* is left until the last two paragraphs, and the sales message is reiterated in the P.S. Notice that most of the preceeding letters contained one or two postscripts. Traditionally, the postscript in a letter was used so that writers could include something they forgot in the body of the letter; a last-minute suggestion or an afterthought. Today, however, it has become a potent sales tool and carrier of a message. Mail-order writers use it to make a final point or to take a last-chance thrust at making the sale. It may contain a special discount "if you order today," or it may say something about "limited supplies" in order to spur the reader to take action.

Mail order, however, is not the only place for using a postscript. It can be used on all forms of business correspondence, including memos. For example, collection letters might include a P.S. that reiterates a benefit to the debtor for paying promptly. Nonetheless, the P.S. should be used judiciously.

PRONOUNS AND WORD CHOICE

Another sales writing tool is the use of the word *you* versus *we*. *We* is an overused term and nebulous. Who are "we?" Are "we" the employees of the company? The letter writer? Both? Use *I* where appropriate and whenever possible. Also, writers of good sales letters use *you* when addressing the reader. It makes the letter more personal, and the readers relate to it.

Sales letters also avoid indefinite terms and dates. They do not use terms such as *not if, may, hope*, and *I trust*, which are all indefinite terms. In order to get a reader to take action, the terms should be definite, the instructions explicit, and the choices limited.

SALUTATIONS AND CLOSINGS

Any discussion of winning structure would not be complete without addressing salutation, spelling, and form. Obviously, salutations can take many forms:

Dear Sir:

Dear Madam:

Dear Ms.:

Dear Sir/Madam:

To Whom It May Concern:

Letter writers, however, should make every effort to avoid using the preceding five salutations. In today's market, personalization is critical. People value their names, and when a letter comes addressed to someone by name, it automatically gets more attention. Think of yourself. When you get a letter at home that is addressed to "occupant" versus your name you open the personalized envelope first. Why? Because we all attach more importance to our names. The same is true when writing business letters. Make every effort to find out the person's name before mailing the letter. The minute or so of effort it takes may pay off with a sale, an open door, or a request that is answered immediately.

If it is impossible to determine a name, you may use one of the aforementioned five salutations. However, be careful when addressing a letter, "Dear Sir" or "Dear Madam." Unless you know for sure that the person is a man, do not address it, "Dear Sir," and unless you are certain that the recipient is a woman, do not use, "Dear Madam." The days of addressing correspondence "Dear Sir" are long gone. More than half the work force is female, thus there is more than a 50–50 chance the person getting your correspondence is going to be female. Many frown on being addressed as "Dear Sir" when they aren't.

If there is no way of determining whether your recipient is a man or a woman, address it, "Dear Sir/Madam," which is becoming the acceptable method.

Also, many recipients of salutations have titles. If so, use them. For example:

Dear Dr. _____:

Dear Mayor _____:

Dear Senator _____:

  or Dear Senator:

Dear Professor _____:

Dear Father _____:

Dear Justice _____:

   or Dear Mr. [or Ms.] Justice:

If there is a question on any of the preceding, use "Dear Sir/ Madam." As for closing letters, there are numerous techniques, such as the following informal choices:

Best regards,

Sincerely,

Cordially,

Sincerely yours,

Cordially yours,

Gratefully yours,

These closings are appropriate when a friendship or relationship exists between the writer and the recipient. For letters between two people who are not acquainted or for whom the business relationship is formal, the closing should be formal:

Yours very truly,

Very truly yours,

Respectfully,

In today's environment, however, the line between formal and informal is, at best, thin. Letter writers should be using the closing that makes them feel comfortable. If an executive is writing a follow-up letter to an executive at another company, there is nothing wrong with using "Sincerely," "Best regards," or some other familiar form. Leave formal closings for letters to people that you have never previously communicated with or do not know.

Although almost any close is permissible, one structural mistake that dooms a letter almost from the start is a typographical error (i.e., a misspelled or crossed-out word). Just as you view correspondence with mistakes of that type as careless and indicative of the type of work the writer produces, so do others. Typos are damaging, sometimes deadly. The prudent executive reviews correspondence carefully before it is mailed. Even if his or her secretary or assistant ranks at the top of the class, the originator of the correspondence should take a minute to carefully reread the document. It is amazing how many times even the best secretary or assistant will err.

CHAPTER **4**

How to Say It

As per your request of your memo dated November 15, 1989, I have completed a thorough market recap for June 1, 1988 through June 15, 1988, and I have come up with information that will give us greater insight into our position in the marketplace and our planning for the coming year.

KEEP IT SHORT

Any writer who takes 60 words to say what could be said in 20 is wasting time—both the writer's and the recipient's time. Good writing does not need to fill the page. More important than quantity is quality. The rules for quality prose follow:

1. Keep it short and simple; as short and as simple as possible.

2. Use everyday language. Do not go to the thesaurus to find three- and four-syllable words when one-syllable words will suffice. Do not coin new words or use acronyms that will confuse people.

3. Write as if you are addressing one person, not an entire room. Keep it personal.

4. Use AIDA (see Chapter 3) to keep you on track and make sure the letter hits home.

5. Keep sentences short and conversational.

Letteritis, or the excessive use of words in letters, attacks many businesspeople. Oddly, most of the people who are afflicted with it are capable speakers when they can communicate face-to-face or one-on-one. Give them a pen, however, and a simple message turns into:

> Per your request for the extension of your loan dated July 5, 1989, our board has taken the matter under submission and consequently decided that the extension will be granted with the proper additional sum of interest to be charged.

Why not . . .

> We are pleased to tell you that your loan extension has been granted. The paperwork will be in the mail within the

next week, and it will reflect the new due date, as well as the interest to be charged.

Some of the most common, inane phrases in letters and memos are listed in the first column of the following table. Compare them to the simpler versions in the second column:

Why	Why Not
during that time	while
after very careful consideration	after considering
be cognizant	know
as of this date	now
during that time period	then
make an examination of	examine
this is a subject that	this subject
the fact of the matter	the fact
make inquiry regarding	inquire
inoperative	doesn't work
at this point in time	now
subsequent to	after
very good	good
brand new	new
be in receipt of	get
at an early date	soon
whether or not	whether

TALKING IN PRINT

Letter and memo writers also tend to use the following formal phrases, although they never use the same constructions when speaking:

as per our agreement

as stated previously above

attached hereto

due to the fact that

enclosed please find

favor us with your reply

hereby do advise

herewith you will find

I beg to advise you

I have your letter of [*date*]

in compliance with your request

in connection therewith

it was carefully noted

it was duly noted that

may we suggest that

per our records

please accept

please be advised

please find enclosed

please rest assured

pleasure of a reply

pursuant to our conversation

regarding said order

regret to advise you that

regret to state that

soliciting your indulgence

the contents were duly noted

with your kind indulgence

with your kind permission

your valued patronage

yours with respect to same

The formal and verbose phrases can be made worse when letter and memo writers also suffer from padding sentences and from being redundant. See how much clearer the following sentences would be if the underlined words were removed. At the same time, the removal would not change the meaning of the sentence. In fact, it would make it clearer.

- It happened <u>at a time</u> when we were <u>all</u> busy.
- <u>The</u> Nintendo <u>game</u> is being sold for <u>a price of</u> $90.
- We are <u>in the process of now</u> building a new facility.
- It happened during <u>the month of</u> August.

- The department will ship the merchandise <u>at a</u> later <u>date</u>.
- In <u>the state of</u> Massachusetts.

Excess verbiage such as the preceding examples would not occur if letter and memo writers would edit sentences, try to make them as short as possible, and keep the four-step writing process in mind.

LETTERS FROM SALESPEOPLE

Thinking about the process is especially important to salespeople who work with the written word in order to increase postpurchase sales (i.e., repeat business).

In today's marketplace, salespeople have less time than ever to spend on clients. Still, communication is important. Some companies estimate that as much as 50 percent of all sales are generated from repeat business. Much of the communication is generated through a series of letters that are sent to customers on a regular basis following their initial purchase.

Ideally, the letters should go every six to eight weeks. That keeps the company (and the salesperson) in the customer's mind. The letters that are sent are seldom pitches for more business. Most of the time, they contain useful information that the customer would like to have. For example, George Cole works out of the corporate office of a firm that specializes in marketing expensive materials to real estate brokers. Cole does most of his work on the telephone, he visits prospective clients at conventions and works through the mail.

Just over a year ago, he put together a series of mailings that go out every seven weeks to previous customers. They are informational pieces. His beginning-of-the-year mailing, usually includes a forecast on the industry and where it is going. The note that accompanied this year's mailing read as follows:

Dear   :

It's hard to believe, but 19— is here!

I just happened to get a copy of the recent [*organization*] study that forecasts real estate activity for the coming year.

Notice that it looks extremely good in the coming months.

Hope the forecast is right on . . .

Sincerely,

George's second mailing (about 6–8 weeks later) may be entirely different. Last year, he sent the following:

Dear   :

We all want to increase sales, and I thought this article would be a real plus for your office.

It details, step-by-step, how salespeople should be working the telephone in order to increase their listings.

Best

A third mailing hits 6 to 8 weeks later. George's mailing included the following:

Dear   :

As a sales tool, you might want to show prospective buyers the forecast I ran into the other day from [*bank*].

It projects that interest rates and home loans are going to be up 1/2 point next quarter, so maybe this is the best time to buy . . .

Could be an aid with the buyers . . .

Best

Notice that George never asks for an order. He is giving information at no cost, which is the key to postpurchase selling; supplying valuable information instills a feeling of gratitude in the customer. By communicating on a regular basis, George is no stranger to the real estate people. Contrast his communication with a competitor who may only visit the real estate office once—to make a sale. When George does make his pitch, the buyers are willing to listen.

George does not waste the customer's time. His notes are short, to the point. George's letter is similar to the message sent by a doctor to the local community (Letters 4–1 and 4–2). In both notes the doctor offers information at no cost.

An accountant came up with a variation of this idea (Letter 4–3), as did a financial planner (Letter 4–4). Letter 4–5 is generic and can be used by any professional.

Dear   :

You may be unfamiliar with me, but I'm familiar with your community. Many people in this neighborhood are more concerned about maximum physical health than in other parts of our city. Why? Maybe they enjoy life more fully; maybe they already keep themselves in better health; maybe they treasure their bodies. Many of them come to see me and have asked for ways in which they can enhance their health. As a result, I've developed a report that you might profit from called [*name*]. I'd like to send it to you. If you're already comfortable with a physician in the neighborhood, I'd still like to send it to you if you'll send back the enclosed card. If you don't have a physician, come to my office anytime and I'd be glad to give you the report.

In the meantime, although I have a busy schedule, if I can answer any questions I'll certainly find the time or have my assistant respond. If there's anything I can do for you, please call.

Letter 4–1: A letter from a doctor offering a free report to members of the community.

Dear   :

   I've just presented a seminar at the local community college on the subject of cancer prevention. One way, of course, is to have regular check-ups by a physician you trust. Another is to modify your eating habits. But there are many other innovative approaches that most people never think about.

   I've taken a liberty that I hope you'll appreciate. I've included a portion of the seminar text here. You might enjoy reading it. If you would like the complete text, call or come in and we'll give it to you.

   This report presents some ideas, techniques and therapeutic methods which will enhance the quality, length and gratification of your life. It's my gift to you. If I can ever be of service in any way I hope you'll call or visit my office.

Letter 4–2: A letter from a doctor including a portion of a report to pique the recipient's interest.

Dear   :

A person in your income bracket may have more complex financial needs than you recognize. Perhaps your current accountant hasn't realized or hasn't pointed out some additional services you could benefit from. Perhaps he hasn't shown you ways you could save on taxes. Perhaps he hasn't suggested tax-saving strategies that others in your income or professional group are currently taking advantage of. I am always disappointed when professionals only react and don't take the time to care about my needs ahead of time.

Come [*date*], all the recommendations in the world won't help. The time to develop your tax strategy is right now. I have an advantage. My practice is busier than can be in November and December; right now I have free time.

If you'd like, I'd be willing to spend an hour or two with you for a modest consultation fee (or for free, depending on what you want to do). We would examine your financial situation and review your last year's taxes; I will ask you a number of questions and, moreover, recommend some strategies. I'll do it as a service to you. I would be delighted if you wanted to retain me after the consultation, but don't feel obligated.

I've helped many people in situations similar to yours and I believe I could help you. Maybe more than your present accountant, maybe less. I don't know for certain but I would be willing to spend the time to see if I could. If I can help you, it could represent thousands or tens of thousands of dollars that you can put in the bank; money you could save, money you could invest, money you could enjoy. And it may change your entire thinking about tax planning and investments.

I have some innovative ideas that are absolutely legal and ethical but are much more dynamic than those of most accountants. My practice has grown because of these ideas. I'd like to share them with you if you're interested. If you are curious, call or send in the enclosed card. My secretary will get back to you. Or come in at your convenience. But because I have a very variable schedule, I suggest that you arrange an appointment.

Letter 4–3: A letter from an accountant offering a low-cost (or free) consultation.

Achieve financial independence in the next 20 years

PLUS

Five easy ways to overcome money problems

For the rest of your life

Dear   :

The headline of this letter may sound audacious but frankly, it's true. As a practicing financial planner in this city for the last ten years, I've been able to show 500 of your neighbors and friends ways, means and techniques that have allowed them to structure a financial plan that will assure them of all the money they want for retirement—or for vacations, for business investment, for a comfortable cushion of money in the bank, for their children's education, or for the exciting luxuries that they have dreamt about.

I often achieve these goals without changing a person's lifestyle in the least, most often with dollars normally paid to the government through innovative tax-sheltering strategics. Most people have no real financial plan and don't understand that, for no more money than they already spend on taxes, they could create more than a nest egg—they could create financial independence.

I've prepared a report entitled [*title*]. I'd be delighted to send you a copy or to sit down with you and explain my techniques in person.

My practice is located at [*address*], which is very convenient. I keep normal business hours and am also available for evening and weekend consultations. If you don't have time for a personal consultation, I would be glad to show you a simple way to create your own financial plan. I have a form that's very easy to fill out which I'll be glad to send you as well.

Enclosed is a card. Send it back to me and my assistant will send you the form and the report. Afterwards I'll follow up and see what I can do for you.

In the meantime, if you have questions or if I can be of any help, feel free to call me with no obligation.

Letter 4—4: A letter from a financial planner offering a free report.

Dear   :

My name is [*name*]. I'm a [*profession*] in your community. I
have developed a substantial practice. My clients enjoy receiving
the [*publication*] that we publish. It's informative, interesting
and helpful. We've enhanced people's health (or financial, or
legal situation); we've been told that people have [*benefitted by*]
using it.

I don't know if we could help you, too, but I thought you
might enjoy reviewing a copy [__ copies]. It's valuable and, I
believe, warrants your spending five, ten or fifteen minutes
reading it. Most of all, I hope it makes you reflect.

After reading it, if you feel that I could be of service to you, I
would be delighted to discuss your particular situation. Arrange
an appointment and I will be glad to confer with you for half an
hour free of charge to see if I can be of service. At that time I'll
tell you some of the things I've done; about some of my past
cases and about my philosophy.

In the meantime, I publish several [*reports, booklets, tapes*] on
subjects of interest to people like yourself. I've listed them on
the enclosed card. If you'll send it back, I'll send you any one of
them with my compliments. I hope I can be of service to you,
and I also hope that what I have already included can benefit
you.

Letter 4–5: A generic letter offering a free publication.

LETTERS FOR SIMPLE TO COMPLEX SITUATIONS

Letter writing style will vary from situation to situation and depending on the writer's relationship to the recipient; but all letters follow the same basic rules presented in this book. The letters in this section range from a humorous, personal note, to a simple cover letter, to a letter to the President of the United States. Although you couldn't possibly use all of these letters, some of them will be right for your situation.

Humor can go a long way in getting and holding the recipient's attention, but be careful how you use it! If you don't really know the recipient or if you are writing concerning a serious subject, the humor will probably not be appreciated. Letter 4–6 is from a banker to a customer whom he or she knows well. The customer needed an amount deducted from a checking account to pay for interest charges. The banker did it with the customer's prior knowledge, but was not able to tell the customer exactly when the withdrawal would occur. Consequently, the banker sent the humorous letter.

This same banker sent another familiar customer a financial statement to sign and submit (Letter 4–7). Both letters show what can be done with a little creativity.

Letter 4–8 shows how a sense of urgency can be conveyed, in this case from a marketing consultant to a client, by presenting the reader with a time limit.

Though sales letters certainly play a crucial (and perhaps underrated) role in business, many other kinds of letters must be written each day. For example, Letters 4–9 through 4–14 illustrate responses to inquiries and to other contacts with clients.

Letters 4–15 through 4–17 show alternative ways in which an organization can try to attract a nationally recognized speaker to a meeting of some kind.

Clearly, there are letters for any kind of situation (Letters 4–18 through 4–26 are a few diverse examples.)

Dear Fellow Banker:

In a last frantic effort to protect your fiscal creditability, I have taken the liberty of charging your account for interest due on August 8, 1985 A.D. in the amount of $1,274.66.

Tried to reach you personally, however, as usual I found you underground.

If you have any question, just call.

Letter 4–6: A humerous letter to a familiar client.

Dear   :

Since I am, as you know, renowned for my fiscal expertise as well as numerous other qualities, I beg your attention. Enclosed you will find a rather formal-appearing document. Be not alarmed, for it is more harmless than it appears.

Historically, such writings were disguised to permit certain knowledge to be imparted to a second interested party. Over the years the nomenclature financial statement was adopted and the usage continues to this very day. Please complete said document and arrange for transport back to this tabernacle of monetary excellence.

Your Humble Servant

Letter 4–7: The humor in this cover letter to a financial statement comes from its excessive formality.

Dear Colleague:

I am writing this letter in an urgent attempt to reach you. Your response must be made within [*seven*] days. I am hoping this letter reaches you in time because I have been unable to reach you by telephone.

Recently, I have formed an association with three multimillionaire business and marketing experts, and together we have developed a pilot program which will allow you to receive our help. Some of the participants who are chosen will be totally inexperienced, some will be intermediate, and some will be experts in real estate and/or entrepreneurial businesses. But all must be very serious about financial success. If you are chosen to participate in this pilot program, you will be given personal consulting assistance to help you, on a step-by-step basis, to establish and reach your financial goals during the next six months.

This consultation service will last for six months and will provide you with creative in-depth investment and marketing strategies which can be tailored to your particular needs.

I hope this letter reaches you in time, because it is critical that you respond immediately. If you have a serious interest in achieving financial freedom within the next six months through this pilot program, please contact me by using my toll-free number which I have installed right in my office for this purpose: [*telephone number*].

Letter 4–8: An urgent plea from a marketing consultant.

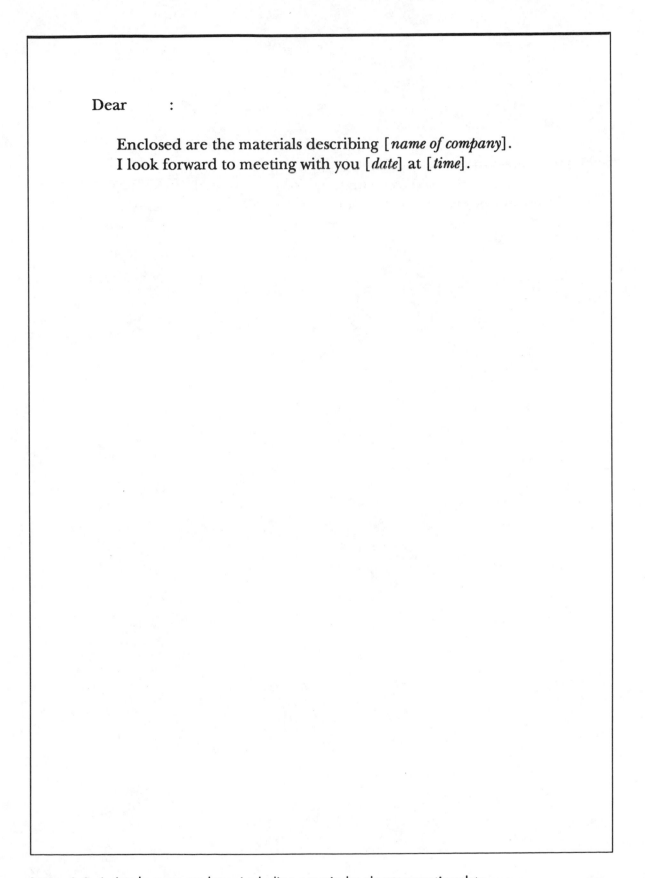

Dear   :

Enclosed are the materials describing [*name of company*].
I look forward to meeting with you [*date*] at [*time*].

Letter 4–9: A simple response letter including a reminder about a meeting date.

Dear   :

Thank you for your inquiry about [*name of project*] and your interest in [*name of company*].

I have enclosed some material for your perusal. If you have any questions, please do not hesitate to call.

Letter 4–10: A generic response letter.

Dear   :

I enjoyed the [*breakfast*] we had together. It seems that yesterdays become today before we know it. I am enclosing material on [*name of company*], so keep us in mind.
I wish you success with your current challenge.
Give 'em hell.

Letter 4–11: A personal letter as follow up to a meeting.

Dear   :

I enjoyed having the opportunity of meeting you last week and mutually sharing our perspectives on the value and delivery performance of [*information systems*] organizations. I always gain insight from such discussions and hope I was able to reciprocate.

Based on [*name*]'s suggestions, I have enclosed some information on [*name of company*]. We believe that by combining [*name of company*]'s leadership capability in the [*information technology*] field with [*name of company*]'s historically outstanding business consulting practices, we will be able to better serve our clients.

I look forward to the potential of working with you and [*name*] in the future.

Letter 4–12: A more formal letter to follow up a meeting.

Dear   :

    I enjoyed the opportunity of meeting with you and partaking in some lively and interesting discussions on the state of [*information technology*].

    Enclosed is a copy of the book, [*title*], which we briefly discussed. I think you will find it interesting. I have also enclosed some material on [*name of company*] for your review.

    If we can be of any help in assisting you in achieving your goals at [*name of company*], please call.

Letter 4–13: A letter sent with various enclosures as follow up to a meeting.

Dear   :

It has been some time since we talked, but I wanted to stay in touch and let you know that we would still be very pleased to present our qualifications and capabilities to [*name of client's company*].

To reacquaint you with [*name of company*], I have enclosed a booklet entitled [*title*], a corporate brochure, and some selected articles.

[*name of company*] has worked with some of the largest corporations in the country, advising them on how to use [*product or service*] to restructure their business processes, and has become noted for turning around and repositioning troubled [*information systems*] organizations.

I would very much appreciate the opportunity to meet with you, or anyone you might suggest, to discuss how [*name of company*] might be able to support [*name of client's company*].

Letter 4–14: A letter to reacquaint a previous client with the company.

Dear   :

It was a pleasure talking with you the other day.

As you requested, I've enclosed materials on our organization as well as our First Annual National Convention.

The [*name of company*] First Annual National Convention in [*city*] was well received by our 1,000 brokers, managers and sales associates. The excitement in part, was due to the dynamic presentation of [*name*], our keynote speaker.

We are anticipating an attendance of over 2,000 for our Second Annual National Convention at the [*hotel*] in [*city*]. I've attached our tentative agenda which outlines our preferred time for [*name*]'s speaking engagemen. Should our opening General Session [*day, date, and time*] not be convenient for [*name*], we would be amenable to [*his/her*] speaking on [*date*], [*a half-hour presentation between 1:30 and 3:30 P.M.*].

As we discussed, [*name of company*] is prepared to offer [*name*] [*$ dollars*] for [*his/her*] speaking engagement either on [*date*] or [*date*]. Since you quoted me a fee of [*$ dollars*] for a one hour presentation, we feel the [*$ dollars*] for a half hour presentation is a fair offer.

We would be pleased to donate [*his/her*] honorarium to [*name of organization*] on [*his/her*] behalf. Should [*he/she*] accept, the donation would of course remain in the strictest of confidence.

Should you have any questions, please do not hesitate to call me at [*telephone number*]. I look forward to receiving your favorable reply in the near future.

Letter 4–15: A formal letter to attract a keynote speaker.

Dear   :

    I am delighted to learn that there is a possibility that you will be willing to deliver the keynote address at our first annual National Convention. Not only would I be pleased to have you as our speaker, but I personally look forward to the prospect of being able to meet you.

    The Convention will be held in what I understand is one of your favorite spots—[*city*]. The beautiful [*name of hotel*] will be the site of our [*three-and-a-half day*] Convention. So far, our roster of speakers includes [*list of names, titles, companies, and accomplishments*]. I'm sure you would be pleased to be in the company of these dignified guest speakers.

    Our company [*company background for a sentence or two*]. Your name has come up frequently in conversations with our affiliates and without question you are their unanimous choice as keynoter.

    [*Name*], our Convention will run from [*date*] through the [*date*]. We would prefer to have you in the classic keynote position as the closing speaker during our last general session, the [*afternoon*] of [*date*]. Please respond at your earliest convenience as we would like to be able to finalize our plans well in advance.

Letter 4–16: A more informal approach to inviting a keynote speaker.

Dear   :

Congratulations on your two remarkably successful terms as President of our country. There is no doubt that history will regard you as one of our country's truly great leaders.

One of the things you did during your Presidency that none of us will ever forget is the way you elevated the spirit of the entire nation. Next [*month*], we will be assembling a group of entrepreneurs upon whom we believe you could have a similar influence.

The occasion is [*name of company*]'s Second Annual National Convention, to be held at the newest and most luxurious hotel to ever be built in [*city*], [*name of hotel*].

We would like to invite you to deliver the Keynote Address at our opening General Session on [*date and time*]. Last year, [*name*] was the Keynote Speaker for our First Annual National Convention. [*name*] set a high standard of excellence for headliners which few, aside from yourself, could match.

The [*year*] Convention will be a historic one for [*name of company*]. A total of more than [*4,000*] [*entrepreneurial real estate*] professionals are expected.

A group of highly distinguished Americans will be joining us for the occasion and addressing the group as well. They include [*name, title, company, and accomplishments*]. In addition, [*name*], the extremely successful head coach of [*name of team*] will address the delegates at our closing General Session.

If you would like to discuss our request or if I can personally answer any questions, please feel free to call on my private line [*telephone number*].

Letter 4–17: A letter requesting a keynote address by the president of the United States.

Dear   :

The coffee is terrific . . . at least that is what we keep hearing from our guests.

It has been a few months now since you first installed our coffee brewers and I am truly remiss in not writing you sooner regarding the success of the program.

Since the first day of installation, the response of our guests has been only positive. I personally have had numerous guests go out of their way to tell me how pleased they are with the added amenity.

With the ever-increasing competition in our marketplace, it is a constant challenge to stay one step ahead of other area hotels. Now, thanks to your wonderful brewer, we are once again the first to step out and provide not only an additional service but one that is useable and therefore perceived as tangible and valuable. I knew that while we were the first, we will by no means be the last. I am sure it will not be long before all of our area hotels, as well as hotels across the country, catch on to the value of this program and that is as it should be. It is long overdue for the hotel industry to re-evaluate their in-room amenities program. Today's traveler is looking for dollar value more than ever before. Therefore, the quality and usefulness of the amenities has become of greater issue to the decision maker.

Through ongoing communication with our guests, it was determined that one service the majority would enjoy was the ability to have fresh brewed coffee at any time they desired.

After much research and evaluation of available coffee systems, we were at a loss. Nothing seemed to quite fit our needs. Then we met with you. I can't thank you enough for all of your help. You took an idea and developed a program that has served to go beyond our original expectations.

Once again a very sincere "Thank You." It is professionals such as yourself and [*name of company*] that make my job easier. All of us at the [*name*] look forward to a long and successful business partnership.

Letter 4–18: A thank you letter from a hotel to a vendor of coffee brewers.

Dear   :

Thank you for the lead from [*name of company*]. As things turned out, they wanted us to testify on behalf of one of their clients. We had to refuse for a strange reason—one of our consultants is testifying on the opposite side.

I do, however, appreciate your referring [*name of company*], and I encourage you to keep doing so.

Letter 4–19: A letter thanking another company for a referral.

Dear   :

I received a copy of [*name*]'s letter recommending our firm as a company that could more than adequately handle the evaluation of future computer systems for your company. As a means of introduction, I have enclosed information about our firm for your review.

[*Name of company*] has worked with many organizations in determining future direction of computer systems, including hardware and software evaluation and selection. We look forward to the opportunity of being of service to you.

Letter 4–20: A letter to a company to which the writer's company has been recommended.

Dear   :

I know you are very busy, as am I.

I also know that as a member of the [*Varsity Huddle*], we are very close to success on our campaign.

I recently had a discussion with [*name*] concerning the status of the campaign, and [*he/she*] advised me that we need a final burst of energy to make it successful.

Both you and [*name*] are a critical link in this process. The [*function*] you have agreed to host may be the single most important element of our campaign strategy.

It is vital that this [*function*] be carefully planned and implemented as quickly as possible.

The stakes are too high to risk a loss of momentum brought about by lack of a sense of urgency. The leadership that you and [*name*] have demonstrated in this campaign is truly worthy of the respect of anyone associated with [*name of organization*]. We do need, however one more push from everyone involved in our campaign to realize success. Which brings me to the tree you and [*name*] now have sitting in your offices. There is an old Latin saying; "IN ARBORESIS NON CRESIS," which means, "It Doesn't Grow On Trees." I think it is particularly appropriate to our campaign. All of us on the "tree brigade" can put this campaign on ice.

Just give your Varsity Huddle this one final extra effort.

Letter 4–21: A letter encouraging a final push in a campaign.

Dear   :

[*name of company*], after 12 years in the business, has achieved another milestone. In order to bring expanded and broader capabilities to our clients in tying information systems technology and business practices together, [*name of company*] has elected to become part of [*name of company*].

[*name of company*] is a 62-year-old international management consulting firm whose practice was originally founded on production and engineering consulting in manufacturing-based industry. In addition, today clients include service organizations, government, and health care institutions. Practice areas encompass strategy, technology assessment, organization, executive search, productivity, marketing and sales, manufacturing, plant engineering, environment, logistics, transportation, and information systems. [*name of company*]'s mission is to help clients improve and maintain a competitive position.

[*Name of company*] will lead the development of a strong, value-added Information Technology Group within [*name of company*]. Our desire is to offer clients an alternative to the Big 8 with broader and more penetrating capabilities.

Letter 4–22: A letter announcing a merger.

Dear   :

At this time of the year, we reflect upon those special people whose advice, friendship, and support we value so highly. At [*name of company*], we appreciate your contribution to our success as a company and as individuals, and we are grateful to you.

May you have a wonderful Holiday Season and prosperity throughout the coming year.

Letter 4–23: A seasonal letter expressing gratitude for continued business.

Dear   :

When I analyze the qualifications of applicants for a sales position, I am primarily interested in their track records—that is, results! Our results are something we can certainly be proud about.

We have been in business since [*year*] specializing in commercial property. We watched the skyrocketing prices of residential property in the late 19__s and questioned ourselves more than once as to whether we were on the right track with commercial properties.

We are now one of the most successful national real estate firms in the country. And, by specializing in the commercial property area, we have become a leader in the real estate field.

I look forward to meeting you and finding out more about your real estate career goals.

Letter 4–24: Recruiting letter from a real estate firm to a prospective salesperson.

Dear   :

    We have been following the newspaper ads you've been placing in order to sell your business. Our company, which specializes in commercial real estate, would like the opportunity to meet with you to see if we might be of assistance.

    We are business brokers and have established relationships with many brokers throughout the country. Our contacts and the advertising that we do enables us to find buyers who are anxious to purchase a business such as yours. These buyers may live in a different part of the country or may simply live in an adjacent county and do not subscribe to the [*name of paper*] in which you are advertising. There are also many individuals who prefer to approach a seller through a broker.

    Selling businesses is our only business. I'll be calling you in the next day or so to see if we can set a mutually convenient time for us to explore the possibilities of our company handling the sale for you.

Letter 4–25: Introductory letter that picks up on an advertisement the recipient placed in a newspaper, and attempts to generate a sales appointment.

Dear   :

I am in receipt of your letter of [*date*] and must say that I was most distressed at its content. I do appreciate your contacting me with regard to difficulties you incurred during your [*month*] visit to our hotel. I wish I could have been aware of your situation during your stay. I would have liked the opportunity to have corrected the matter for you at the time.

From what you have told me, it appears that one problem created another with regard to the heating system that would not work because you could not close the balcony door completely. With regard to the roaches, I must tell you this is a problem we have been working to solve since our renovation. It does not reflect poor housekeeping; rather, it reflects the problem of a fourteen year-old hotel that had never had carpeting or vinyl replaced. It is not a problem unusual for Southern California hotels, but it is one that can normally be controlled and kept out of the way of our guests.

I understand your feelings with regard to our hotel, but I would like to think that one day you would come again and allow us the opportunity to be of service in a manner that would benefit your requirements.

You made a statement that you would never again take a room at a [*name of hotel*]. I hope that you would have taken the time to think about that as there are many wonderful [*name of hotel*] throughout the world, and I would not like to think that your experience with us would prohibit you from experiencing the fine hospitality of so many good hotels.

Once again, I do appreciate your constructive criticism and because of it, future guests will benefit. It is my sincere wish that you will be one of them.

Letter 4–26: An unintentionally humorous letter in response to some understandable complaints. Although the customer is probably too upset to ever return, it is still best to respond to the complaint, and to respond honestly.

MEMOS

The following memos are interesting because they show the points of view of three different companies.

The first (Memo 4–1) concerns the merger of a company and the additional personnel that have joined the firm. The approach is interesting and poses a challenge for employees in the firm.

The next concerns credit procedures (Memo 4–2) and it is followed by memos concerning salary (Memo 4–3), vacation time (Memo 4–4), an audit (Memo 4–5), and new personnel (Memo 4–6). A company's personality is often revealed in its memos. Can you guess how many of these memos came from the same firm? Which belong together?

(Answer: Memos 4–2, 4–3, and 4–4 were from the same company. Memos 4–5 and 4–6 came from the same firm. Memo 4–1 was from a third company. Note the similarity of the first firm's memos in their harsh tone.)

Avoiding Negativity

A golden rule that applies to memos as well as letters is that they should never be negative. Certainly, there is room for criticism in a memo, however, the criticism should not be aimed at any one person. Criticism should take the form of creative suggestions rather than a critique of someone's performance or department.

How you say it may not only affect your job, but it also affects the way people view you. A manager who sends a memo to the field will have an image among field people long before he or she ever visits it.

Sample Memos for a Variety of Situations

Memos 4–7 through 4–18 were gathered from the personnel and sales department of a northwest U.S. manufacturer, and a southeastern clothing distributor.

```
DATE:

TO:

FROM:

SUBJECT:    New Information

We are extremely excited about the potential
of our newly formed [name of group].

To further acquaint you with the key
individuals from [name of company] that are
now part of our Firm, enclosed are their staff
resumes. Also, in an effort to quickly
identify a portion of the "value added" that
each of the new people bring to our new Group,
we have prepared a list of their professional
staff and the special skills/experience each
person contributes.

In addition, enclosed is [name]'s book
[title]. It is a summation of representative
client activities over the years, as well as
[name of company]'s view of the future
direction of the information systems field.
This may help you to understand their focus in
the marketplace.
```

Memo 4–1: A memo covering new information about a merger.

DATE:

TO:

FROM:

SUBJECT: Changes

Instead of billing all credit card customers
when we receive the order, today we begin
billing when we ship the products. This may
result in the customer being charged on their
credit card more than once since we ship in-
stock items immediately with rings shipped
later.

Also, we are reducing our liberal 40 day
return policy to a "strict" 30 days. The only
exceptions to this will be 1—if the 30th day
falls on a weekend, it will be extended to the
following Monday; and 2—if UPS or the Post
Office takes longer than ordinary to deliver
(usually a week in each direction), in which
case we will calculate the delivery time in
each direction and add 10 days for the
customer to examine the product.

We have discovered what we believe is causing
our high refund rate, which jumped from 6%
last July to 24% currently. The back side of

Memo 4–2: A memo announcing a new credit policy.

our collate or packing slip actually
encourages and instructs the customer to
return the product. Effective today, no
packing slip will be included in the package
until we have new ones printed without the
instructions.

These policy changes should result in fewer
refunds, customer complaints, less charge-
backs and less work for several departments.

Add this to your policy and procedures book.

Memo 4–2: *(continued)*

DATE:

TO:

FROM:

SUBJECT: Salary

Hourly employees in this department are
expected to cover the store on Saturdays
during the non-holiday season. Each employee
will take the day in rotation, as planned by
the customer service manager.

Since you will be receiving commission on your
sales in the store, there will not be any
overtime paid for the Saturday store day, only
straight time. However, we expect that when
you do not have customers in the store, you
will work on customer service paperwork.

Memo 4–3: A memo outlining specific points regarding hours and salary.

```
DATE:

TO:

FROM:

SUBJECT:    Vacation time

As of now vacations must be taken between
[date] and [date]. In the past we have given
all new employees a week's vacation during
their first year even if they have not earned
it by being here a year. If someone left
before their first year they were charged back
for the unearned vacation time.

Because of the confusion surrounding this
policy, we have decided to change it to an as
earned policy.

In other words, if you started in March and
want to take your vacation in June, you have
earned 3 months toward your vacation. So we
would pay you for 1/4 of one week's pay as
vacation. If you started in November and want
a vacation in August, you will have earned 10
months toward a week's vacation and will be
paid for 5/6 of a week's pay, or 83%.
```

Memo 4–4: A memo about vacation time.

You may take the remaining days of your week off without pay or come back to work. You must take your vacation within the year. You cannot accrue it.

If you do not wish to take a vacation, you will be paid for the days earned, if approved by management.

Employees here over one year will not be affected by this change.

If you have any questions contact your supervisor. Any supervisor who has a question contact [*name*].

Memo 4–4: *(continued)*

DATE:

TO:

FROM:

SUBJECT: January Audit

I have been informed that auditors from the
accounting firm of [*name of firm*] will be here
[*time, date*] to inspect our inventory. In
preparation for this, please be prepared to
show the auditors your physical inventory.
They will want to count and inspect items to
assure that the items listed are indeed on
hand and accurately accounted for. We may also
have to document the original purchase price.

This is a very important function of our
fiscal year close, so please help by being
well prepared. Please see me if you have any
questions.

Memo 4–5: A memo announcing an audit.

```
DATE:

TO:

FROM:

SUBJECT:    New Employee

The capabilities of the Marketing Department
have been further enhanced by the addition of
[name]. [name] is a public relations
professional with over 25 years of experience
in [his/her] field. [He/She] has worked with
franchisees, has spent considerable time
involved with entrepreneurs and has,
therefore, some excellent tools to bring to
the franchise industry. [He/She] has also
worked with a variety of show business
personalities.

[Name] lives in [city] with [his wife/her
husband] [name]. [He/She] is an alumni of
[school] and a devout [team] fan. [He/she]
also is the author of five books.

We have looked forward to having [name] on
board and are very glad that [he/she] is here.
Feel free to give [him/her] a call or drop in
on [his/her] office and say "hello."
```

Memo 4–6: A memo announcing a new employee.

```
DATE:

TO:

FROM:

SUBJECT:    Roles and Responsibilities

From what was said in our meeting this
morning, Fred _____ will be responsible
for _____, John _____ will handle
_____, and Mary _____ will be in
charge of _____. Fred will chair the
three-person committee and report to the
executive committee on its activities.

The committee will meet monthly, with the next
session on [date] at [time] in the conference
room.
```

Memo 4–7: A memo issued following a meeting, which outlines duties and responsibilities of the people attending.

DATE:

TO:

FROM:

SUBJECT: Today's meeting

In our two hour meeting, the pros and cons of introducing the new line in March versus June was thoroughly discussed, and we unanimously voted to move the introduction to March.

The reasons for the move: (1) we beat the competition (2) we make use of down time in our southeast plant (3) none of us believe the fashion/style season has firm dates anymore— and the first one out there with the best gets the most.

Harry _____ will take care of gearing up the plant, Fred _____ will talk to our designers and order fabric, John _____ will meet with the marketing and sales department and plan the early intro.

The committee will meet two weeks from today in the board room to report progress.

Memo 4–8: A memo reiterating a discussion in a meeting.

```
DATE:

TO:

FROM:

SUBJECT:    Accounting report

We checked the accounts at northeast region
with Sally _____ and found the region had
spent $20,000 on 19__ real estate forecasting
reports. The contract is firm and it runs for
two additional months. The payment has been
made so there are no further funds due. Sam
Esplanade originally made the purchase and
received an ok from our corporate treasurer,
Manfred Adams.
```

Memo 4–9: A memo from accounting to a vice president to report on a specific expenditure.

```
DATE:

TO:

FROM:

SUBJECT:    Timetable for Ad Campaign

Our first quarter 19__ campaign kicks off the
second week in January which means we have a
firm timetable that all of us have to follow.

The week of August 10, we have to finalize ad
plans and media for the campaign. Let's plan
to meet in my office Tuesday, Aug. 11 at 9 A.M.
The first week of September, we have to
present the plans to each of the seven
regions. Joyce will confirm the dates with
each region and give them to you by August 1.

If there is a question about the schedule,
call me ASAP.
```

Memo 4–10: A memo from marketing to the ad agency that is handling the account.

```
          DATE:

          TO:

          FROM:

          SUBJECT:    New medical insurance program

          Many of you have asked about a major medical
          program, and I am happy to say we now have
          one. It is being provided by [company] and the
          benefits and costs are listed on the enclosed
          sheet.

          After you examine the costs and benefits, you
          have the option of having it deducted from
          your paychecks or paying quarterly in advance.
          If you decide you do not want the plan, that
          is acceptable as well.

          I spent time looking through the plan,
          comparing its costs and benefits to others,
          and I can tell you for our company this is the
          best plan available.

          If you have any questions, [name] in personnel
          [telephone number] has the information.
```

Memo 4–11: A memo announcing a new insurance program.

```
DATE:

TO:

FROM:

SUBJECT:    Christmas hours

Ho! Ho! Ho!

. . . and merry Christmas from [company].

In celebration, President [name] has decided
that we will close early on the 23rd (3 p.m.)
and will have the 24th off to spend with our
families.
```

Memo 4–12: A memo announcing an early closing.

```
DATE:

TO:

FROM:

SUBJECT:   Food in the refrigerator

Help!

We need your cooperation.

The refrigerator in the kitchen has numerous
food items that have been there for some time
and should be removed.

We will be housecleaning next [date] at [time]
and at that time everything in the
refrigerator should be removed and taken home.
Anything that remains will be discarded.
```

Memo 4–13: A memo regarding "housecleaning." (Note: when making this type of request, humor may help to prevent employees from resenting management.)

```
DATE:

TO:

FROM:

SUBJECT:    Time for blood donations

Good news!

Each year we work with the Red Cross in
setting up a special room for blood donations
from employees. This year the one-day drive
kicks off after lunch on Friday and will be
held in the main conference room on the fourth
floor.

As a bonus, [name], our President, said that
anyone who donates can take the rest of the
afternoon off!

Call [telephone number] for an appointment and
take Friday P.M. off with pay . . . .
```

Memo 4–14: A memo soliciting blood donations.

```
DATE:

TO:

FROM:

SUBJECT:   Data processing shut down

Be prepared. That's not only the Boy Scout
motto, but it also applies to [corporation]
next [date].

At [time], we will be turning off all the data
processing equipment for a housecleaning. Be
sure and log off before [time]. Any documents
you have that have not been logged off could
be lost.

If you have a problem or question, give me a
call at [telephone number].
```

Memo 4–15: A memo notifying employees about a specific event that may concern them.

```
DATE:

TO:

FROM:

SUBJECT:   Employee departure

It is with regret that I announce the
resignation of [name] as [position].

[name] has been with us for more than [years]
and [he/she] will be taking on new
responsibilities at [company], which is
considerably closer to [his/her] home.

[He/She] will, however, be with us until
[date]. After that, we'll all miss [him/her]
but wish [him/her] the best in [his/her] new
position.
```

Memo 4–16: A memo concerning an employee who is voluntarily leaving the company.

```
DATE:

TO:

FROM:

SUBJECT:    New employee

Effective immediately, [name] has left our
company and is no longer [position].

[Name] has been appointed the new [position]
and has assumed [his/her] duties immediately.

Any questions relating to [department]
projects or procedure should be addressed
directly to [name].
```

Memo 4–17: A memo announcing a change of employees. (Note: Although the departing employee was dismissed, it is never directly noted.)

```
DATE:

TO:

FROM:

SUBJECT:   Congratulations

Bravo!

What more can I say. Your efforts at the
recent convention were superlative. And
without question, everyone in attendance
learned something because of the time and
effort you put into the organization of the
event.

I'm looking forward to next year's convention
and know with you in charge it will be another
outstanding event.

On behalf of the company and everyone in
attendance, my congratulations for a job well-
done—as usual.
```

Memo 4–18: A memo congratulating employees on a job well done.

USING "CC AND "BCC"

Whether you are writing a letter or a memo, one other element should be kept in mind—letter and memo writing can be political, especially in a corporate atmosphere. Far too many people have found themselves out of a job because of carelessly sending a memo over the boss's head while not sending a copy to the boss. (The designation "cc:" for carbon copy originates from the carbon paper used for this purpose.) Also, several executives have found themselves at a dead end with a firm because of a careless note or memo about the chief executive officer (CEO) that found itself in the CEO's hands.

If the project involves your department, always make sure your boss has a copy (cc:). Also, memos can help to clarify a situation in which someone is about to take the blame for something that he or she had nothing to do with. A well-written, documented memo to the responsible party, with a cc: to the boss or even a memo directly to the boss, may come in handy. Also, on occasion, it is appropriate to use "bcc" (blind—meaning that the recipient does not know about the carbon copy).

CHAPTER **5**

Problems
and
Solutions

Happy birthday and all the best . . . even if you are a
little more than mature.

I have heard a lot of speeches—good, bad, and
indifferent. Yours was none of the three . . . it was
superb.

All letters are solutions to specific "problems" or situations. For example, contrast the two brief notes on the first page of this chapter. Obviously, the congratulatory note could be sent to a variety of people following a speech. But the birthday greeting only fits a few; those who are a few years up the ladder (and who don't mind admitting it). Clearly, not every letter or memo suits all recipients, all writers, or all situations. For this reason, you will find a variety of different letters and memos for all occasions in this chapter. Though many apply to the same situation, they vary in approach and will give you the opportunity to select the letter or memo that best fits your situation.

MEMOS FOR MANY OCCASIONS

The first 15 are customized memos. Memos 5–1 through 5–3 offer appreciation for employee suggestions, Memos 5–4 through 5–6 extend thanks and congratulations to employees, and Memos 5–7 through 5–10 offer ideas for motivating employees. (Memos 5–9 and 5–10 might be sent from a senior executive to those in the field to let them know how things are going, in hopes of inspiring them.)

Often, memos are intended to seek or to offer advice. Memos 5–11 and 5–12 might be sent between a key executive or manager and another officer of the company whom the executive respects.

Other memos are intended to remind employees about company policies and procedures (Memo 5–13).

Some memos must advise employees of the unpleasant results of fiscal difficulties. For example, it is exceedingly difficult to tell employees that they are not going to get a Christmas bonus, especially if they are used to receiving something. Memo 5–14 has the wording that can help because it gives the employees the reasons that they are not getting a bonus.

```
DATE:

TO:

FROM:

SUBJECT:     Suggestion

Your suggestion that we create an incentive
for customers to upgrade their computer system
has been taken under consideration. We have
decided to offer owners of the system a [$
dollar] rebate, when they trade their current
one in for a higher priced unit. We are
preparing the announcement for dealers and
will inform all of our customers shortly.

Your idea was superb and in recognition of it
you will find a check for [$] enclosed.
```

Memo 5–1: A memo acknowledging the suggestion of an incentive program. (Note that the monetary gift noted here and in Memo 5–2 will not always be appropriate.)

```
DATE:


TO:


FROM:


SUBJECT:    Suggestion


It was with a great pleasure that I learned
today of the acceptance of your idea to start
[project].


It is truly an excellent idea and will prove
very beneficial to the company. The speed with
which it is being implemented indicates the
value of your suggestion.


Congratulations, once again. We're extremely
impressed. Enclosed you will find a check for
[$ dollars] in appreciation of your idea.
```

Memo 5–2: A memo acknowledging the suggestion of a project.

DATE:

TO:

FROM:

SUBJECT: Suggestion

Your suggestion that we recycle the trims from
our vinyl production has been analyzed and it
is an extremely viable idea.

This recycling process, which will be
implemented in six to eight weeks from now,
will result in direct savings to our firm. We
commend you for your inventiveness!

Please accept our congratulations on the
adoption of your recommendation and our thanks
for your enthusiastic attitude.

Memo 5–3: A memo acknowledging the suggestion of a money saving innovation.

```
DATE:

TO:

FROM:

SUBJECT:    Thank you

You are to be highly commended for the way you
handled the emergency that occurred yesterday.

The paramedics have informed us that if you
hadn't acted as quickly as you did, our
customer's attack might have been fatal.
Thanks to your fast reaction, [he/she] is
already out of intensive care and on the road
to recovery.

I am extremely proud of your actions and of
your association with our company.
```

Memo 5–4: A memo thanking an employee for handling a medical emergency.

```
DATE:

TO:

FROM:

SUBJECT:    Congratulations

You have proven the skeptics wrong and
accomplished what most said was impossible.

There is no doubt that your recent
achievements will be spoken of for some time
to come and that the admiration for your
accomplishments is felt by all of us within
the industry as well as the general public.

Please accept my heartiest congratulations for
your success.
```

Memo 5–5: A memo of congratulation for a specific job well done.

```
DATE:

TO:

FROM:

SUBJECT:    Congratulations


[date] marks your [fifth] anniversary as a
member of the [name of company]. I would like
to take this opportunity to thank you for
these past [five] years of fine workmanship
and company loyalty.

The growth and success of our company is
largely dependent on having strong and capable
staff members, such as yourself. Your
contribution has helped us attain the position
we enjoy in the industry.

On behalf of the company, we hope you will be
with us for many years to come and would like
to offer our congratulations on your
anniversary.
```

Memo 5–6: A memo congratulating an employee on a company anniversary.

```
DATE:

TO:

FROM:

SUBJECT:    Thank you

Thanks [name] and all the other people working
at [name of company] for a job well done
during the past year and most especially
during the Christmas rush.

I appreciate the diligence, work ethic,
courtesy and cooperation that you have
displayed to our customers.
```

Memo 5–7: A thank you memo for a job well done.

DATE:

TO:

FROM:

SUBJECT: Invitations/Donation

On [*date*], at [*time*], in the employee
cafeteria, there will be a retirement party
for [*name*]. As you know, [*name*] has been with
the company for __ years, and has done an
outstanding job.

We would like to get [*name*] a retirement gift,
and if each of us donates [*$*] we can present
one befitting the time [*he/she*] spent with the
company.

We are undecided on the type of gift, and your
suggestions are therefore encouraged.

Look forward to seeing you at the party.

Memo 5–8: A memo announcing a retirement party.

```
DATE:

TO:

FROM:

SUBJECT:    Progress

This past year has been a difficult one, but
thanks to you we were able to come through it
in much better condition than we originally
thought.

In the months to come, I feel confident that
you will continue to perform in a manner that
will result in an increase in sales and
commissions that will far exceed our
projections.

With your help, the outlook for the coming
year is brighter than it has been for some
time. With a positive, assertive attitude,
nothing can stop us!
```

Memo 5–9: A memo to motivate employees to achieve peak performance.

DATE:

TO:

FROM:

SUBJECT: Motivation

There are always the prophets of doom and the
cynics who will be happy to lead their
followers through long periods of drought and
famine.

When an unfortunate individual starts blaming
his own failures on others, and on conditions
over which he has no control, he can usually
forget about achieving his goals.

There are good times and bad times, but at all
times there are sales that are made and sales
that are lost.

You have all proven that you are not only
capable, but also excel as salespeople. I am
proud of the accomplishments of our sales
force and know that nothing can hold back the
motivated individual who has an excellent
product to sell.

Memo 5–10: A memo to inspire a salesforce.

```
DATE:

TO:

FROM:

SUBJECT:   Advice

Frankly, I need your advice on a matter of
great concern to the employees at the local
manufacturing facility. Constant rumors of a
corporate takeover are filtering down to the
general work force, and the loyalty is
faltering. I have heard some employees are
submitting their applications to our
competitors. This could, of course, create
problems.

I feel obliged to make some sort of official
statement to the employees and hope for your
guidance as to the content thereof.

I would be most grateful for your thoughts and
advice on this most sensitive matter.
```

Memo 5–11: A memo seeking advice from a respected coworker.

```
DATE:

TO:

FROM:

SUBJECT:   Suggestions

The anxiety about the proposed merger is
affecting my department. The memo put out last
week did little to assuage the fears of
employees. It might be helpful to meet the
issue head-on by holding a meeting so
questions can be posed and answered.

The rumors are creating a schism between
employees and management. If the merger fails
to materialize, the employees could maintain
their current feelings of alienation to the
company.

I know there are problems in having the
subject out in an open forum, but they should
be weighed against the present feelings of
employees.
```

Memo 5–12: A memo offering a suggestion.

DATE:

TO:

FROM:

SUBJECT: Expense

It is essential that any of our personnel who
use an automobile in connection with company
business maintain a thorough record of the
expenses incurred. It is our desire to be
certain that you are reimbursed for any
expenditures that you make in this regard, and
your good recordkeeping will make this
possible.

Receipts must be submitted for expenses,
repairs and parking. In addition, we will
require your daily record of the number of
miles driven, the odometer reading, before and
after, and the amount of time spent driving.
This information should be contained in your
weekly report to [name].

Thank you very much for your cooperation in
this matter.

Memo 5-13: A memo reminding employees about a travel expense policy.

```
DATE:

TO:

FROM:

SUBJECT:    Christmas bonus

This has been a difficult year for [name of
corporation]. I am sure that you all know that
the loss of our three contracts with the
United States Air Force, due to the cut-back
in defense appropriations, hurt us
substantially.

In July, we had a major decision to make. The
question we were faced with was whether to let
some of our employees go, or to explore all
other possible avenues of cost reduction,
keeping everyone's job intact. We chose the
latter course. Unfortunately, one of the
policies we were forced to eliminate for this
year, was our annual Christmas bonus to each
of our employees.

This will be the first year since [year] that
we will be unable to thank you in this special
manner for your hard work, loyalty and
faithfulness. We are all hoping that [year]
will be a prosperous year and that we will be
able to reinstate our traditional Christmas
bonus policy.
```

Memo 5–14: A memo announcing that a Christmas bonus will not be forthcoming.

Even more painful is advising employees of layoffs. Word-of-mouth almost always precedes a layoff memo. A memo such as Memo 5–15 would normally be delivered by a supervisor and not just handed out. It, too, should have rationale as to the reasons for the layoffs.

LETTERS RESPONDING TO CUSTOMER ORDERS

Letters in response to customer orders can cover a wide range of topics between a company and persons outside the firm. Letters 5–1 through 5–6 present various responses to customer orders.

COLLECTION LETTERS

Collections are tricky. Companies to not want to alienate clients, but sometimes, harsh letters have to be sent. Letters 5–7 through 5–17 offer a wide variety of choices, from very mild to harsh.

Letter 5–18 takes a different approach. This company wants to avoid late payments by offering a discount for early payment of accounts.

Letter 5–19 shows how someone might respond to an overdraft resulting from a bank error.

OTHER DIFFICULT LETTERS

Other letters may also require great tact. For example, Letters 5–20 and 5–21 show ways in which customer complaints might be handled.

Letter 5–22 illustrates a way in which to inform customers of a price increase.

LETTERS REGARDING CHARITABLE CONTRIBUTIONS

Letters of Request

Letter 5–23 shows an appeal for a charitable contribution, and Letter 5–24 suggests how to handle a delicate situation in regard to a request for charitable contribution.

```
DATE:

TO:

FROM:

SUBJECT:    Layoffs

We had been hoping that during this difficult
period of reorganization we could keep all of
our employees. Unfortunately, this is not the
case. Aside from the two recent [contracts,
clients, etc.] we lost, there is one other
contract that will [leave or expire] at the
end of this month.

It is with regret, therefore, that we must
inform you that we must cut back and we will
be unable to utilize your services after
[date]. We have been pleased with the
qualities you have exhibited during your
tenure of employment with us, and will be
sorry to lose you as an employee.

Please accept our best wishes for your future.
We are hoping it will be much brighter than
the past few months.
```

Memo 5–15: A memo announcing layoffs.

Dear   :

　　We received your order for [*item*] and wish to thank you.
　　This item however, is presently on back-order and we are unable to ship it. We hope to have it in stock by [*date*].
　　Please accept our apology for this inconvenience and you may expect delivery in approximately [*time*].
　　If you have a question, please call our special order-inquiry line. It's toll free [*telephone number*].

Letter 5–1: A response to an order that could not be immediately filled.

Dear   :

We are happy to inform you that the parts you ordered are now in stock and available for pick up at the above address.

Please accept our sincerest apologies for the delay in delivery and we thank you for your patience.

If we may be of further assistance, please feel free to call on our toll free line, [*telephone number*].

Letter 5–2: A notice that previously ordered items are now available for pick up.

Dear   :

    We received your Purchase Order Number [*number*], dated [*date*]. However, part of your P.O. cannot be filled for the following reason: [*reason*].

    Please call [*number*] so we can straighten out the problem. The balance of your order should be to you by [*date*].

    We look forward to your future orders and are ready to assist you in any way possible.

Letter 5–3: A response to a purchase order.

Dear   :

We appreciate your order, however, there has been a problem in fulfilling. The terms and conditions on page [*233*] of our catalog specify that overseas orders are only accepted with full payment in advance, plus with an amount sufficient to cover shipping.

Therefore, we are unable to ship until either a sight draft, or an irrevocable letter of credit is received. We anticipate shipping charges to be approximately [*price*].

May we please hear from you as soon as possible.

Thank you for your order. I look forward to hearing from you soon.

Letter 5–4: A letter addressing the problem of improper ordering procedures.

Dear   :

Due to the huge response we received from our summer catalog, we are experiencing a delay in filling some of the orders. Item [*number*] should be sent to you within [*time*] from this date.

Please accept our apologies.

Letter 5–5: A letter apologizing for a delay in delivery due to unexpected demand.

Dear   :

I received your letter acknowledging receipt of the items we mailed to you and requesting us to cancel the back-ordered items.

I've done that and will be issuing you a refund as soon as we complete the necessary paperwork.

I would like to thank you for shopping with [*name*] and apologize for the back-order situation. Our new catalog should be arriving at your home shortly, and I believe you will be pleased by some of the beautiful choices our buyers have made.

Thank you again for your patience and understanding and for providing us with the opportunity to be of service to you.

Letter 5–6: A response to a request to cancel back orders.

Dear   :

   Last [*day*], we discussed the past due balance on your
account. At the time you said a check had been put in the mail.
It has been several days and we have not received the check.
   In light of that we are holding all orders until a check arrives
and the past due balance is cleared. I regret to say that we
cannot fulfill any new orders.
   If a check has been mailed, please accept our thanks. If not,
please call immediately so we can clear the matter up.

Letter 5–7: A collection letter in which the company explains it will hold all orders until payment is made.

Dear   :

    As one of our most valued accounts, it is with regret that I must tell you we have had to change the credit on your account because of past-due balances.

    From now on a check must accompany each order for merchandise. This will be in force until your account is brought up to date. At that time we will reevaluate your status.

    We value your business and hope that this will not interfere with our long and profitable relationship. We look forward to resolving this matter. Please call me by [*date*] so that we may clear things up.

Letter 5–8: A collection letter using a change in credit policy as incentive.

Dear   :

I have written you on several occasions requesting an explanation as to why your account has not been brought up to date.

By ignoring these requests, you are damaging the excellent credit record you have previously maintained with our company. In addition, you are incurring additional expense to yourself and to us.

Unless we hear from you within ten (10) days, I will have no other choice but to turn your account over for collection. I am sorry that we must take such drastic action, but I am afraid you leave us no alternative. You can preserve your credit rating by remitting your check today for the amount stated above.

Letter 5–9: A collection letter using the threat of turning the bill over to a collection agency.

Dear   :

All of our efforts to settle your account amicably have been unsuccessful. We have made numerous calls and, to date, you have not called back. We have delayed legal proceedings based on your assurances that the bill would be paid in full by [*date*]. I am enclosing copies of your letter stating that intention.

Please be advised that you have left us no alternative but to file suit immediately. We have attempted to be understanding of your cash flow problems, but our patience has now reached an end.

Your account is being turned over to our attorney. While I regret the necessity of this action I must advise you to govern yourself accordingly.

Letter 5–10: A letter stating that the account has been turned over to an attorney for legal action.

Dear   :

    Your account is seriously past due, however, we have valued your business for many years, and hope that this lack of payment is an oversight. If payment has been made, thank you. If not, please advise this office if any discrepancy exists. We have reviewed your account and must at this time cancel existing credit lines unless payment is received within ten days.

    I understand that you have had problems lately, and feel that we have been most accommodating. Accordingly, I will expect your check no later than [*date*].

Letter 5–11: A sympathetic but unyielding collection letter.

Dear   :

Approximately eight weeks ago we shipped [*product*] to your firm. As you know, this was the first purchase you charged to your new account.

We are, of course, pleased to have you as a new customer and are looking forward to a long relationship. However, this will only be possible if we honor our commitments to make delivery when promised and you honor your commitment to remit payment in a timely manner.

We have honored our part of the agreement, and we are asking you to please follow suit by placing a check for [*$ dollars*] in the enclosed envelope. If there is a problem, please call us by [*date*] so we can resolve it.

Thanking you in advance for your prompt attention to this matter.

Letter 5–12: A collection letter that relies on reasoning.

Dear   :

    As a good businessperson, I know you are aware of the manner in which seriously past due accounts must be handled. I am not going to attempt to think of some clever phrase to get your attention. Nor do I wish to embarrass or intimidate you to encourage payment.

    I am merely informing you that your account has reached a point where we must decide by [*date*] whether to turn it over for collection or just hand it to our attorneys, neither of which is our preference.

    I hope you understand our predicament. Please call before [*date*] as to your intentions.

Letter 5–13: A collection letter that addresses the recipient as an adult who does not need to be cajoled or threatened.

Dear   :

Our firms have been doing business together for a long time. That is why I cannot understand why you have not responded to our reminders about your past due account.

I'm here to listen if you are experiencing a problem and we are anxious to retain the goodwill we have shared over the years.

I am not even requesting your payment at this time, but merely asking you to contact our credit manager to discuss your bill and any extensions you might need.

Please, let us hear from you soon.

Letter 5–14: A collection letter to another firm with which the company has had a longstanding relationship.

Dear   :

Just a friendly reminder that some of your charges have gone beyond our regular terms. The overdue items were listed on this month's statement for your convenience.

I realize you do business with various suppliers and it may be difficult to process invoices for payment on the due date. However, I've enclosed a copy of your statement so you can review your past due invoices. Now that you can review them, won't you please authorize a check to cover them.

Thank you for your cooperation.

Letter 5–15: A "friendly reminder" giving the recipient the benefit of the doubt.

Dear   :

I have been notified by our credit department that your account is past due. Because you are one of our preferred customers, we would like to offer any assistance we can. I know most overdue balances result from clerical errors. However, if you require additional time to pay please call. I am authorizing an additional [*number*] days in which to pay your remaining balance.

I value your business and sincerely hope this extra time will solve the problem. We look forward to hearing from you soon.

Letter 5–16: A letter granting a certain number of extra days in which to pay.

Dear   :

We are interested in our customers and are always trying to find new ways to improve our service. For these reasons, we are inquiring as to the delay in your payment.

As you know, your account is [*months*] overdue. If we can help by giving you smaller monthly payments and extending the terms, please let us know. You are a valued customer and we hope in working together we can take care of this matter.

We would appreciate hearing from you by [*date*] as well as receiving at least a partial payment.

Letter 5–17: A collection letter that suggests various solutions, such as extending credit terms and accepting partial payment.

Dear   :

Did you know you could have saved [*$ dollars*] last year?

That's right. In the past twelve months you have purchased a considerable amount of merchandise from us, for which we thank you.

However, you have never taken advantage of the [*2%*] discount we offer for early payment. We thought that you might be unaware of just how substantial your savings could be. The savings on last year's purchases alone would have amounted to [*$ dollars*].

By paying us within ten (10) days of delivery, you can actually save [*24%*] of the face amount of your average monthly bill over the period of a year. There are, in fact, firms that prefer to borrow funds to take advantage of this discount and we want to be sure that you are aware of this savings factor.

Also, we would like to take this opportunity to thank you for the orders you have given us over the past year.

Letter 5–18: A letter offering a discount for early payment.

Dear   :

 When I received your letter with my check attached marked "insufficient funds," I called my bank immediately.

 I discovered the bank had failed to credit my account with a deposit.

 I wish to apologize, and the bank has assured me it will send you a note of apology for its error. Attached is my check in the amount of [$ *dollars*] to replace the one returned by the bank.

 Thank you for your patience in this matter.

Letter 5–19: A letter of explanation for a bounced check.

Dear   :

Your note to our General Manager regarding your unpleasant experience at our Christmas dinner was turned over to me. On behalf of the hotel let me take the opportunity to apologize for any inconvenience or disappointment you may have experienced.

We take a tremendous amount of pride in our Holiday Buffets as we do in our entire hotel. It is apparent that on the day you were here we were in error. Whether a guest arrives at the beginning of an event or at the end they have a right to expect the finest and the freshest. Apparently this did not happen.

At this point to offer you a refund seems very cold and empty. I would instead prefer the opportunity to allow you to experience the [*name*] as it should be, as our guest for either a dinner for six and one child, or a brunch, or Easter Sunday dinner. If you would contact me direct I would be happy to make the necessary arrangements for you.

We want to be sure that as new California residents you come to know that our hospitality can be as warm and wonderful as our climate.

We appreciate your input and look forward to the opportunity to be of service.

Letter 5–20 A letter offering a free gift in reparation for a complaint.

Dear   :

    Thank you for taking the time to fill out the questionnaire during your stay with us. We appreciate hearing from customers, and their comments are vital in order for us to continue improving our accommodations.

    The problems you mentioned have been brought to the attention of our housekeeping department. While the lack of service you experienced is unusual and not the standard for our hotel, there is no excuse for a lackadaisical attitude on the part of any of our employees. I apologize, once again for the inconvenience this incident caused.

    Thank you again for your comments. We hope that you will give us another chance to serve you.

Letter 5–21: A letter in response to a complaint made on a company-provided questionnaire.

Dear   :

Due to the increase in raw material costs, we must, unfortunately, raise the cost of our merchandise to all of our customers.

We have avoided raising our prices for as long as possible, but we can no longer forestall the inevitable. We have enclosed our new price list for your perusal, which goes into effect on [*date*]. Any orders placed between now and [*date of increase*] will be honored at the lower prices.

We wish to thank you for your valued account and know that you will understand the necessity for this increase.

If you have any questions, please call.

Letter 5–22: A letter explaining a price increase.

Dear   :

We are asking for your assistance in helping us in our appeal for contributions.

[*name of organization*] provides shelter, food and donated articles to individuals who have no place to turn in large and small communities throughout the country. All contributions that we receive are used here to help our citizens, whether they live in the Appalachian Mountains of Virginia or in the bustling city of Los Angeles.

We are asking you to help us in our attempt to make life tolerable for these unfortunate individuals and in many cases giving them the incentive to become productive members of society.

Your contribution will be greatly appreciated by us and by all of those who will benefit.

Thank you so very much.

Letter 5–23: A letter requesting a charitable contribution.

Dear   :

Thank you for considering a contribution to [*name of organization*]'s Annual Support Campaign. [*name*] has informed me that you might be willing to make a gift of [*$ dollars*] if, in return, you receive a full facility membership in addition to the considerable recognition given to donors who contribute at this level.

This type of arrangement can be made. However, only the amount of the gift in excess of the value of the membership could be claimed as an income tax deduction. The value of the membership will vary with the category, individual, company, etc.

I'll call to see if you have any questions regarding this arrangement. Again, thank you for considering [*name of organization*]. I look forward to talking to you.

Letter 5–24: A letter offering an added incentive to contribute.

Letters of Appreciation

Letters 5–25 and 5–26 illustrate responses to cash donations. Letter 5–27 responds to the donation of items.

Letters 5–28 through 5–32 show various responses to donations of time, effort, and leadership for nonprofit organizations.

Letters of Inability to Contribute

By far, the most difficult letters to write in regard to charitable contributions are those in which the respondent must confess inability to contribute to a worthy cause. Letters 5–33 through 5–36 show a few ways in which firms have handled this awkward situation.

REJECTION LETTERS

Another awkward situation is posed when a firm must reject someone's services, whether the services are those of an existing supplier (e.g., Letter 5–37), a potential supplier (e.g., Letter 5–38), or applicants for a position within the firm (e.g., Letter 5–39). Letter 5–40 illustrates a tactful way of handling a candidate who is still in the running for a position in which the decision is pending.

THANK-YOU LETTERS

Far more delightful letters—for the writer, as well as for the recipient—are thank-you letters. Many of these can be even more effective if they are handwritten notes. Examples of these include Letters 5–41 through 5–43, thanking the addressee for enjoyable experiences. Letters 5–44 through 5–48 offer thanks for being invited to enjoy an experience; Letters 5–44 and 5–45 accept the invitations and Letter 5–46 graciously declines.

Letter 5–47 thanks a speaker for accepting an invitation.

Another occasion on which a handwritten note seems particularly suitable is when an employee receives a gift of some sort from an employer (see Letter 5–48).

Dear   :

Please accept the enclosed plaque as a token of our sincere appreciation for your generous contribution to our 19— Current Support Campaign. We hope that you will proudly display this symbol of your generosity and membership in this very special group of [*name of organization*] supporters.

In recognition of your gift, your name has also been engraved on the Chairman's Round Table donor wall at [*organization*]. I hope that you will stop by to see it.

Again, on behalf of the thousands of youths, families and seniors whose lives are touched because you care enough to give, please accept our heartfelt gratitude.

Letter 5–25: A letter describing specific forms of recognition for a donation.

Dear   :

On behalf of everyone who benefits from your donation, please accept our thanks for your generous [*$ amount*] gift to our Finish the Job Campaign.

Your gift will go a long way toward helping us to complete our facilities. I will see to it that your donation receives the appropriate recognition. In fact, [*name*] has asked that the [*name of thing or a place, such as a room*] be named in your company's honor. Unless I hear otherwise, I will proceed with [*name*]'s request.

We are deeply grateful and promise to fulfill our commitment to you of providing the best possible [*name of organization*] program to our community.

Letter 5–26: A letter thanking a donor by offering to name something after him or her.

Dear   :

Thank you for your donation of [*item*].

The generous gifts we receive from people such as you make it possible for us to continue the programs and services we offer our community.

Again, our sincere thanks.

Letter 5–27: A letter acknowledging the donation of a certain item.

Dear   :

Just a note of appreciation for the extraordinary leadership that you have given and are giving to our Major Gifts campaign.

The recruitment phase of our campaign was completed in a most successful fashion as a result of your efforts, and the solicitation phase of the campaign is off to an excellent start.

I thank you for your willingness to lead this effort and to make and keep [*name of organization*] strong.

I'm looking forward to our continued work together and to a successful conclusion to our efforts.

With appreciation and admiration,

Letter 5–28: A letter in appreciation of leadership efforts.

Dear   :

Now that your term on the [*name of board*] has ended, please accept our appreciation for your time of service. [*name of organization*] works best when a true working partnership between staff and volunteer leaders is achieved. Your being a part of that partnership has been important to the advancement of the [*name of organization*] program, and for that we are thankful.

We hope that you will continue to support the [*name of organization*] program, as the needs of those we serve never go away. Just as your role in the development of [*name or organization*] is appreciated, so will your future support be valued.

Letter 5–29: A letter of appreciation to a departing volunteer leader.

Dear   :

Just a note of sincere thanks and appreciation for the year that you served as President of [*name of organization*].

The goals of [*name of organization*] were advanced during your term, and life in our community has been enriched as a result of the service done by [*name of organization*] under your leadership.

We're grateful for your willingness to put in the time and effort for our community. I'm looking forward to our continued association.

Letter 5–30: A letter thanking the retiring president of an organization.

Dear   :

Just a note of thanks and appreciation for your outstanding leadership and work for this year's annual [*name*] campaign.

I know that the spectacular results are probably rewarding enough, but I wanted to tell you that we appreciated your willingness to take on the challenge of leading the 19__ campaign. Leading the campaign is certainly not an easy job. We are grateful for your help. I am very proud of the results, and I thank you for your willingness to give of your time and talent.

Letter 5–31: A letter acknowledging leadership of a specific project.

Dear   :

   With the completion of your term on our Board of Managers, I want to thank you for the time and talent that you have given to advance the goals of [*name of organization*]. We have made considerable progress and achieved much in recent years, and that is in no small measure due to the support of a group of outstanding volunteer leaders. On behalf of the thousands of youth, families and seniors that have benefited from a strong organizational program, please accept a heartfelt thanks.

   To formally express our appreciation, please accept this invitation to attend our Annual Meeting and Volunteer Recognition Dinner scheduled for [*date*], at [*time*]. At that time we would like to present you with an award in recognition of your outstanding service to [*name of organization*]. I hope that you'll plan to attend.

   Though you are leaving the board, you know that we'll continue to count on you to support our programs and to help out with projects from time to time. So don't be surprised when you're approached about an occasional volunteer job. We can't afford to let someone with your experience and knowledge of our organization to get off that easily! That's one way to saying that we still need you and have appreciated what you have done. You're still very important to [*name of organization*].

Letter 5–32: A letter inviting the recipient to an awards dinner in honor of volunteer efforts.

Dear   :

    As you know, for many years we have placed orders for program ads for your annual benefit. The work that has been done by [*name of organization*] to provide medical assistance to all of the members of this community is most admirable. It is with deep regret, therefore, that I must inform you that our firm will not be participating in this year's ad program because of budget problems.

    I do want to extend our best wishes to your organization for a successful benefit and hope that you will ask us again next year.

Letter 5–33: A letter blaming inability to contribute on budget difficulties.

Dear   :

    We regret to inform you that we will be unable to contribute to your [*fund/cause*]. Our company policy dictates that we limit our contributions to large multipurpose campaigns. Each year, we cooperate with the employees of our company on a national basis in providing support for the [*United Way*] and the [*National Museum Foundation*].

    By contributing to these organizations, we are able to serve a number of worthy causes without showing favoritism.

    I hope you will understand our position. We all, however, support your goals and stated purpose, and wish you every success in your campaign.

Letter 5–34: A letter in which the reason for not contributing is company policy.

Dear   :

Our firm is a member of various organizations that keep us in touch with general business trends in [*name of city*]. These organizations also enable us to work with other businesses for the common good. While you are to be commended on the formation of [*name of organization*], our firm's full membership in your association would merely duplicate our other efforts.

[*name of firm*] will be most happy to cooperate with you in any manner which does not conflict with our company policy. We extend our best wishes for your success.

Letter 5–35: A letter in which the reason for not contributing is that contributions are already made to a similar organization.

Dear   :

Your request for our support for your 19— campaign has been turned over to me for my attention.

There are, however, so many worthy organizations that seek our help that we have had to develop a policy regarding contributions.

We have a committee that meets [*date, time*] to determine the charities to which we will be contributing. At this time, all of our funds that are available for contributions have been earmarked based on this year's decisions. I am therefore unable to help you in your drive. I will, however, be happy to submit the name of your deserving organization for our future consideration.

Although we cannot give you any financial support, please accept our best wishes for a successful drive.

Letter 5–36: A letter in which a request for donation is denied but which promises future consideration.

Dear   :

In accordance with the terms of our contract with you for [*type of business*] services, this is to serve as a thirty (30) day notice for termination of that agreement. We will expect you to provide service through the [*date and month*]. Final payment for your services through that time will be made following receipt of your invoice. Any costs that we incur for items lost or broken by your crew will be deducted from your final payment.

Please contact me if you have any questions.

Letter 5–37: A letter terminating a service. It should be specific and factual.

Dear   :

    Thank you for the time you spent in evaluating our existing system and the estimate you provided for improving it.

    After considering the proposal and evaluating the cost as well as other factors, we have decided not to proceed with the suggested improvements at this time. We will, however, keep them in mind for possible implementation at some future date.

    Your efforts in this matter are most appreciated.

Letter 5–38: A letter rejecting a service estimate.

Dear   :

Thank you for your interest in [*position*] at [*name of company or organization*]. Although your qualifications came close, we found a number of applicants whose qualifications more closely fit our requirements.

As a result, we have reviewed the applications and have elected to conduct interviews with those candidates whose qualifications more closely fit the requirements of the job.

We appreciate your consideration of [*company or organization*], and wish you all the best in the future.

Letter 5–39: A letter rejecting a job candidate.

Dear   :

    Sorry we have had such difficulty in contacting one another. Rather than continue our game of telephone tag, I thought that I'd send you a note on the status of our selection process.

    We have not yet settled on a candidate. Your application remains in consideration. Several more candidates will be interviewed before we settle on one.

    Please contact me if you have any questions. Your continued interest in [*name of company or organization*] is appreciated.

Letter 5–40: A letter to a job candidate informing him or her of the current status of his or her application.

Dear   :

The dinner you gave for the members of the [*company or organization*] was simply wonderful. The food was delicious, and I can't remember ever having a more enjoyable evening.

Thank you for inviting us to this lovely affair and, of course, as always, you were a charming [*host/hostess*].

Letter 5–41: A thank you note for a formal dinner.

Dear   :

    I would like to thank you and your charming wife for a most enjoyable evening. Not only was the dinner absolutely outstanding, but you also made us feel so comfortable that we undoubtedly stayed much longer than the rules of etiquette dictate. We thoroughly enjoyed every moment.
    Once again, many thanks to a wonderful host and hostess.

Letter 5–42: A thank you note for a more casual dinner.

Dear   :

The speech you delivered at the [*name of company or organization*] dinner was extremely informative and enlightening. You touched on so many critical areas that are of concern to management, that I found myself identifying with each and every problem you presented. In particular, the points you made regarding [*topic*] were definitely helpful.

Thank you for sharing your thoughts and experiences with us.

Letter 5–43: A letter thanking a speaker at a dinner.

Dear   :

    [*Mr./Mrs. name*] and I are looking forward to having dinner with you at your home on [*date*].

    Thank you for your thoughtful invitation. We shall see you at [*time*].

Letter 5–44: A letter accepting an invitation to dinner.

Dear   :

It is with great pleasure that I accept your invitation to address the membership of [*name of organization*].

I would like to speak on [*topic*] if that subject is acceptable to you. Please let me know how much time is allotted for my speech, and the format, if any, you would like me to follow.

Thank you for the invitation. I will be looking forward to going over the particulars with you.

Letter 5–45: A letter accepting an invitation to speak.

Dear   :

Thank you for the invitation to serve on the Affirmative Action Study Task Force. Although I recognize the importance of this issue to our Association, I must decline your invitation. I currently have a number of commitments to [*names of associations*]. My participation in these takes a substantial amount of time and attention away from [*present job*].

Although my branch and I both benefit from my activity with the various committees and groups with which I participate, I have reached a point at which my commitments must be limited. I know that you understand and will feel free to call on me if I may help in a peripheral way.

Thanks again for thinking of me and best wishes with your task.

Letter 5–46: A letter declining an invitation to serve on a committee.

Dear   :

[*name of organization*] is pleased that you have agreed to be the guest speaker at its Governmental Affairs Committee meeting on [*date*] at [*time*] in our [*organization*] offices at [*address*].

Within the [*city*] business community [*subject*] is a "hot" topic about which the business community would appreciate the latest information.

You will be the [*name*] guest for lunch. We suggest your speech be 20-25 minutes, to be followed by a question and answer period. It would be best if you arrived at approximately [*time*].

We would also appreciate your forwarding a biographical sketch in advance of the meeting in order to properly introduce you.

We look forward to your attendance and appreciate your participation in our Governmental Affairs program.

Letter 5–47: A letter thanking a guest speaker for accepting.

Dear   :

    I would like to thank you for the Christmas bonus check that was included with your best wishes for the holiday season.

    In addition to your generosity, I would also like to thank you and the company for providing me with a work environment that lends itself to both creativity and productivity.

    I hope that you and your family enjoyed your holiday. Happy New Year!

Letter 5–48: A letter of thanks from an employee for a bonus.

LETTERS OF CONGRATULATION

Letters 5–49 through 5–56 illustrate congratulatory notes, covering occasions from birthdays and new ventures to retirement. Note that Letters 5–54 and 5–55 also serve as marketing tools for soliciting customers.

CONDOLENCES AND SYMPATHY LETTERS

Sick or injured employees need special handling. Thoughtful managers also send personal notes to the employee—handwritten, if possible (see Letters 5–57 and 5–58).

Anyone writing a letter of condolence realizes that words are often inadequate to convey feelings. Anyone who has had occasion to receive condolences has found that the best letters of condolence state simply and sincerely the writer's true feelings. Letters 5–59 through 5–61 illustrate this, but something so personal should not be taken from a model; they should come from the heart of the writer.

PERSONNEL-RELATED LETTERS

To close out this chapter, Letters 5–62 through 5–65 cover personnel issues that every company faces. Although the formats here are basic, you will often want to elaborate on the employee's history.

Dear   :

    I want you to know that on December 6th at 8:00 P.M. (eastern standard time), I shall be raising my champagne glass and wishing you a very happy birthday.
    May your next year be filled with health, happiness and wonderful surprises.

Letter 5–49: A birthday greeting.

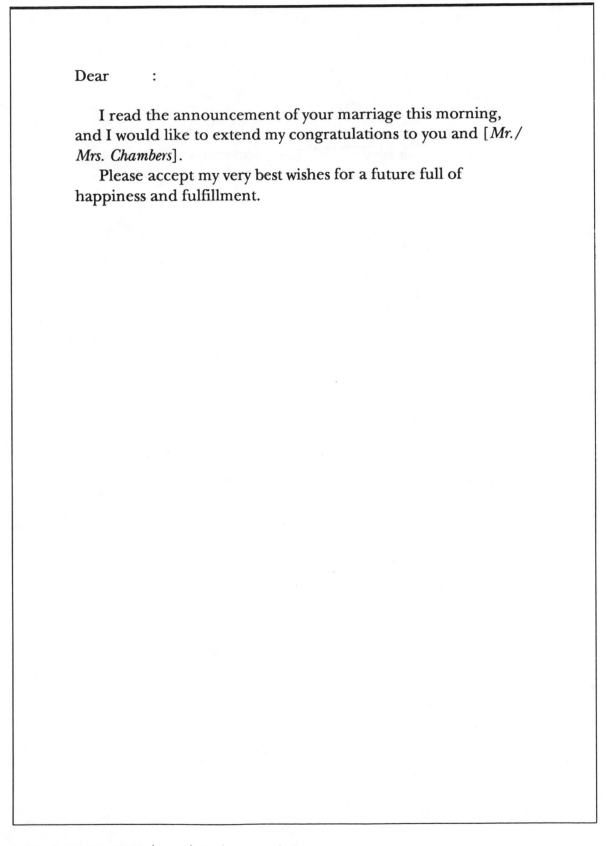

Dear   :

    I read the announcement of your marriage this morning, and I would like to extend my congratulations to you and [*Mr./ Mrs. Chambers*].
    Please accept my very best wishes for a future full of happiness and fulfillment.

Letter 5–50: A congratulatory letter on a marriage.

Dear   :

There is a rumor circulating throughout the office that you have just become the proud [*father/mother*] of a beautiful, baby [*daughter or son, or maybe twins*]. Congratulations to you and to [*Mr./Mrs. name*] on this wonderful and blessed event.

Letter 5–51: A congratulatory letter on a birth.

Dear   :

It was with great pleasure that I read in the evening paper that [*name*] received a [*Rhodes*] scholarship. I know how you have always helped your child[*ren*] strive for excellence in their scholastic endeavors, and I am sure that you must be very proud.

Please extend my warmest congratulations to [*name*].

Letter 5–52: A letter of congratulation on a scholarship.

Dear   :

    Congratulations on taking office as President of [*name of organization*].

    With your leadership, the [*name of organization*] goals will be advanced and the community will be better served by your having taken office.

    Your willingness to give your time to causes that make our community a better place is appreciated by all of us. I am looking forward to our continued association.

Letter 5–53: A letter of congratulation to the president of an organization.

Dear   :

Congratulations on the opening of your new [*type of business*].

. . . and welcome to thc [*area*] business community.

I would like to take this opportunity to introduce you to our business—computers.

Every business requires a good computer system, and we have developed complete programs for all sizes of businesses. While some are more expensive than others, they all have a mutual goal: to save time and money for business.

I have enclosed one of our brochures for your perusal and will call to see if we might be able to arrange a convenient time for one of our systems analysts to meet with you.

In the meantime, best wishes for success.

Letter 5–54: A letter of congratulation on the opening of a new business which takes the opportunity to enclose a brochure.

Dear   :

    Our heartiest congratulations and best wishes for your success in your new enterprise.

    We provide [*type of service*] to many small businesses in the area and will be happy to arrange to have one of our sales representatives call on you at your convenience. I'll call to see when we might be able to arrange an appointment.

    Looking forward to serving you. Once again, congratulations.

Letter 5–55: A letter of congratulation to a new business that sets up a follow up phone call.

Dear   :

   Congratulations and best wishes for your retirement. We commend you for your [*number of years*] of outstanding, productive service.

   Many of your valuable ideas have been adopted by our company. We will surely miss you but know that you will enjoy your leisure. Come see us often; we look upon you as part of our family!

Letter 5–56: A letter of congratulation on a retirement.

Dear   :

Everyone here at [*name of firm*] was distressed to hear of your unfortunate accident. They all join me in wishing you a speedy recovery.

I want you to know that there is nothing pressing here that cannot wait until you are back on your feet again. I hope you will spend the next three or four weeks taking good care of yourself and allowing your body the full time for recovery that is needed. Please be assured that there is nothing more important than your health.

Please let us know if there is some way that we can be of assistance to you during your recovery. Our very best wishes are with you.

Letter 5–57: A letter of sympathy to someone who has had an accident.

Dear   :

   Earlier today, I learned about the accident you suffered last week. I am told that the injury was minor, in view of the possible damage that could have been done.

   I know the employees join me in wishing you a full and speedy recovery. We look forward to your return to work and hope that you will keep us informed as to your progress.

   If there is anything you need, please let me know. I hope to be stopping by to see you from time to time.

Letter 5–58: An alternate approach to a letter regarding an accident.

Dear   :

Please accept our condolences for the loss of your [*relative's relationship*]. If there is anything that we can do for you and your family, please do not hesitate to contact us.

Our thoughts and prayers are with you.

Letter 5–59: A letter of condolence on the death of a relative.

Dear   :

    I was greatly saddened to learn of [*name*]'s death. [*He/She*] was an outstanding individual and was genuinely admired by all of those who worked with [*him/her*].
    Please accept my deepest sympathy and my very best wishes for your future and that of your child[*ren*].

Letter 5–60: A letter of condolence to the spouse of an employee.

Dear   :

    My associates and I wish to extend our deepest sympathy to you and your [*spouse*] upon the loss of your [*son/daughter*].
    Please let me know if there is anything I can do to assist you during this most difficult time.
    With deepest feelings, I am

                           Sincerely,

Letter 5–61: A letter of condolence on the loss of a son or daughter.

Dear   :

    This is to recommend [*name*] for your consideration. [*name*] has worked for [*name of organization*] during the past [*number of years*] as a [*position*]. [*He/She*] has distinguished [*him-/herself*] as a knowledgeable, reliable and personable staff member. [*His/Her*] enthusiasm and commitment to the [*name of field*] has been an inspiration to our [*clients and staff*].

    I can recommend [*name*] for employment with your organization without hesitation. [*He/She*] will be an asset to any organization fortunate enough to have [*him/her*] on staff.

Letter 5–62: A recommendation letter.

Dear   :

In response to your request for verification of employment for [*name*], our records indicate that [*he/she*] worked for us from [*date*] to [*date*].

The position that [*name*] held with our firm was [*position*].

This is all of the information I am able to provide to you inasmuch as it is against our company policy to offer comments in regard to a previous employee's quality of work during employment with our firm.

Letter 5–63: A response to a request for verification of employment.

Dear   :

To follow-up on our recent conversation, I will recommend to our Executive Committee that you be placed on leave from our Board of Managers for [*duration*]. Though we need your help and very much want to retain you as a member of the board, the need for your absence is understood.

The Nominating Committee will meet again in [*month*] of [*year*] and we'll contact you then to determine whether or not conditions have changed. In the meantime, we may need some limited help and will contact you when that occurs.

Your continued interest in our [*name of organization*] and its programs is deeply appreciated. We look forward to the time when once again, you can serve actively on our board.

Letter 5–64: A letter concerning a leave of absence.

Dear   :

    It is with regret that the [*board of managers*] of the [*name of company or organization*] accepts your resignation.

    We have appreciated your affiliation with us and the contributions that you have made to the success of our [*company or organization*].

    We will miss your presence and wish you well as you pursue other interests.

Letter 5–65: A letter accepting a resignation.

Index